S0-AJB-201

Calabrian Summer

Calabrian Summer

BRYN GUNNELL

RAND McNALLY & COMPANY

CHICAGO · NEW YORK · SAN FRANCISCO

DG
975
C15
G8

© *Bryn Gunnell 1965*

Library of Congress Catalog Card Number: 66-23793
*Rand McNally & Company edition, published in the
United States and possessions in 1966*

51920

Contents

Acknowledgments

I am grateful to the following organisations in Rome for supplying statistical information: SVIMEZ; Editoriale di Cultura e di Documentazione; Centro Informazioni Bibliografiche; Istituto Centrale di Statistica.

Illustrations

All these photographs, and that on the jacket (a street in Cosenza), were taken by Louise Gunnell

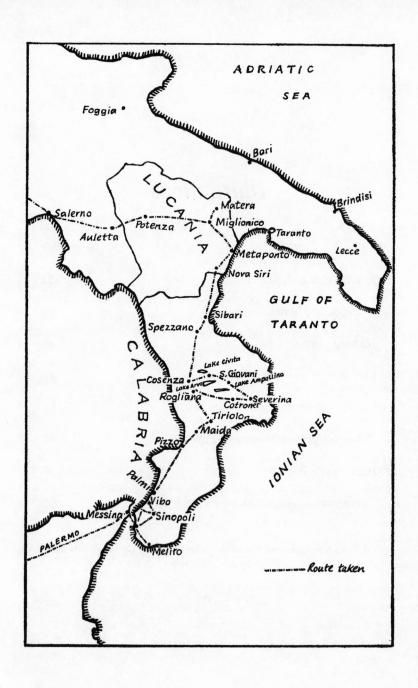

Introduction

'TRAVELLER' is considered an old-fashioned word nowadays: it raises a smile. The traveller has become a tourist, and lost much thereby, and tourist is almost a word of contempt—no one distinguishes between the label and the man beneath it.

People go abroad in increasing numbers every year, convinced that this year's holiday will be more wonderful than any other. They have done Spain and Greece; they have seen all the monuments and read all the guide books; and, once more, they are ready to become victims of the tourist industry. The shiny brochures are irresistible. The seeds of dream have been sown.

I find most historic sites boring and I think it a pity that people feel obliged, out of deference to fashion and taste, to confuse what is old with what is beautiful and to praise everything they see because it is expected of them. Little history is to be gained from a lightning tour round Epidaurus, guide-book in hand. People no longer look with their own eyes or dare to admit what pleases them and, as tourists, they fail to take part, if only for an hour or two, in the daily life of the country they are visiting.

If you want to get to know a region you have to mix with the people living there and try, however gropingly, to understand their mentality. Language is no great barrier. A little goes far, you learn more on the way, and goodwill does the rest. You have, too, to travel slowly, to stop often and savour a landscape, a house or a face.

When my wife and I go wandering—for neither 'tourist' nor

9

'traveller' really fits our case—we go with rucksacks and by any makeshift means of transport that offers itself. The Italians call this travelling by *mezzo di fortuna*, and a happily chosen name that is. Fortune generally succeeds in keeping us off the main roads, and gives us time to stop and stare, to drink and quench our thirst, to hear people out—in a word, to be vagabonds.

In Italy the South is called the Mezzogiorno. If we imagine a line extending from Naples to Pescara in the Abruzzi, the Mezzogiorno includes the whole region to the south and east of it, together with Sicily and Sardinia—all those areas which, economically and socially, form a great contrast with the more prosperous North. It is a problem, the Mezzogiorno. People prefer not to talk about it, as if ashamed of some infirm, unsightly relative, and, from Rome northwards, they look at you in a quizzical way when they learn that you want to see the depressed areas.

What we saw in these parts of Italy is set down here. The whole journey was ruled by the luck of the road.

Part One

CHAPTER ONE

First Encounter

SALERNO is shimmering white and slower in tempo than Naples. There is no port and so the outer world seems more remote, yet it is the last town on the road south which can be called animated.

Our rucksacks brought stares of amazement from the Sunday promenaders. Big-bosomed mothers, showing off their daughters for the benefit of the males of the town, shrank back as we passed, and we left behind us a wake of whispered conferences. Salerno did not detain us long; for us it was a gateway. We camped on the outskirts of the town and, early the next morning, started to walk south towards Battipaglia where we arrived, tired out, under the midday sun.

You cannot really arrive in Battipaglia: you are suddenly there before you have realised it is a town at all. It is characterless and, were it not so sun-drenched in its sleep, it would be simply drab.

But the trattoria near the railway station had character. There was one regular eating his lunch at the blotched table, and the peeling walls and slimy floor were not designed to jog even the healthiest appetite. Kittens ran everywhere—scrawny, wild-eyed creatures that dived in and out of the boxes ranged along the wall where they had made nests among the crisp spaghetti. Tortoises—at least four of them—ambled about the floor, chewed leaves in corners and left ominous puddles. You could not stir your chair without the risk of putting a sudden end to the life of some animal.

After waiting nearly an hour we were served with bitter, inedible spaghetti by a slatternly mountain of a woman and her daughter. The girl, when she was not engrossed in a romantic magazine, tortured the kittens by rolling them over with her feet. There was no meat and no fruit, so we asked for some bread. Mother and daughter rummaged in cupboards full of rusty tins and faded packets, but without success.

At last the meal was over. The women smiled for the first time when we paid, and we went out into the town to look for a café. A few tables and chairs stood in the shade of acacias in a little square beside an imposing school. A dozen boys, aged between sixteen and nineteen, soon gathered at the tables around us, staring and whispering, 'They're foreigners'. One boy with tinted glasses and a brilliant blue suit began to ask us questions and they all edged closer, eager to try out their English and French. Most of them, we discovered, had failed their examinations and were just loafing about, waiting for the next ordeal in the autumn. When not at the café they spent their time racing to and from the coast near Paestum on Vespas or in their fathers' cars. They were quick-witted and curious about everything, but inclined to take themselves very seriously. There is no slow transition in Italian boys: from scruffy urchins they suddenly become perky young men, showy and very careful of their immaculate shirts and shoes.

While we were talking a negro boy joined the group. Several of them openly made fun of him. '*Frutta della guerra*,' they said, shrugging their shoulders and aping his accent. There were shouts of laughter when a ponderous priest went by, accompanied by two acolytes. '*Il corvo nero!*' they chirped. 'He's off to administer extreme unction.'

The table was soon covered with empty coffee cups. The waiter was a boy of about ten, wearing a white jacket which came below his knees, and his eyes flashed fire when the older boys jibed at him. 'He's a student,' they said. 'He's earning money during the holidays to pay for school next year.' Wealthy fathers preserved them from such indignity.

One of their teachers sauntered past, saw the clustered heads and came over to see what it was all about. He taught French, which he spoke with an atrocious accent, and was obviously annoyed by the bubble of youthful spirits around him. He tried to be serious, reeled off lists of authors he had certainly never read, and succeeded only in appearing pedantic and ridiculous. The boys felt this and laughed at him, but he set his face and persisted in expatiating on Claudel and Mauriac. He seemed to have heard only of Catholic authors. He clearly despised the boys and clucked tetchily at them to make them behave. 'Excuse their ignorance,' he kept saying.

Some of them said they would like to learn Russian. 'There you are! Where *do* they get those ideas? I'm very glad nobody teaches Russian in our school.' I suggested it was a beautiful as well as a useful language and that learning it had nothing to do with political views.

'I don't think so. What these boys need is more Latin. When our own civilisation offers so much, why should they want to go dabbling in Slav languages?' He rose to go. 'A private lesson, you know. You must excuse me.'

'Ha!' said one of the boys when he had gone. 'He gives lessons to the daughter of the chief of police!' This kept them chuckling until we decided that it was time, too, for us to go. The boys accompanied us out to the road to Eboli. Glittering eyes followed us as we set off and then, with one great whoop, they all turned, ran down a side street and were lost to sight.

Battipaglia seemed sleepy enough the day we were there, but it is not always so. In late summer, especially, the whole region buzzes with activity, for then the tomatoes are gathered to be pulped and tinned in local factories.

In the last century the plain behind Paestum was malarial and the only inhabitants were the cowboys who herded black buffaloes. Now the whole plain is a single tomato field and one of the few places south of Naples where regular employment is available. Everybody works—often fifteen hours a day—in the height of the season, and the money earned by the seasonal workers has to last the first part of the winter. From January onwards they live on credit—the local shopkeepers rely on their getting work during the next season.

CHAPTER TWO

Beyond Eboli

WE reached Eboli in an hour. The first cool of the evening made walking easier. People were different at Eboli: not so cock-sure and brittle as on the coast. At the baker's a girl was piling the powdered bread with slow, sure movements, and served us with no fuss, no particular desire to please.

At the crossroads below the town we were shown the road to Potenza by a blacksmith who was sitting outside his smithy under some huge plane trees. He looked as though he had always been there, waving people on towards Potenza.

'Where are you off to, walking like that?' he shouted in Italian. 'Calabria! *Madonna, che corragio*! American lorries used to stop here during the war. I got quite friendly with some of the soldiers. I've still got a photograph one of them gave me.' A rasping thumb had left little that was recognisable—a group of round blobs on square shoulders. He grinned and turned it over. It came from some studio in Rapid City. Rapid City is probably no hive of activity but to the Eboli blacksmith it was a dream worth harbouring.

Just outside the town the plain widens for a space and then, to the east and north, the mountains rise suddenly, blue to the north with white towns perched on them, and, to the east, bare and isolated, edging out to the sea.

Near the turning to Campagna we stopped. At a farm—a low-browed white house with a flat roof—we asked for water. A woman came from milking the cows, her head swathed in a white scarf. Her eyes were pure blue in her brown, wrinkled face: her face looked like one bright eye, all sincerity. Her two sons were working somewhere in North Italy and she wanted to detain us, to mother us. 'It is as though they had come back,' she said, but she was obviously so busy that we didn't like to stay long.

A little dry valley among vineyards offered a good place for camping. The stubble fields became dusty gold as the scrub-covered mountains purpled into dusk. A buzzard glided out into the blue and wheeled once more on its last reconnoitre of the day. The cicadas shrilled crescendo as the sun dipped and, once it had gone, fell silent. We sat in the breathing quiet amid the thyme and the rusty tang of vines. A breath of wind from a funnel between the mountains smelt of sere grass and thistles. A flight of plovers flashed past, fluting towards the sea, and suddenly it was night.

The coolness of early morning did not last long. The long blue shadows slithered into gullies all too soon and by eight o'clock the sun had climbed high. We stopped by a roadside spring and waited for a countrywoman to fill the casks her donkey was carrying. The donkey watched the bright water with wondering velvet eyes. The woman, stocky and determined, hitched her skirt over her mud-spattered legs and waited while the jet bubbled and winked into the casks. When they were full we drank and washed. She didn't speak, but she smiled to herself—a little self-satisfied smile—when a passing lorry driver shouted compliments and whistled.

A van stopped. The woman snatched away the casks while the driver doused his head thoroughly. When he had finished he offered to take us towards Potenza. He was lame, with a quiet voice and eyes like a loris.

It was not easy to keep upright in the back of the van on sliding packets of spaghetti and broken biscuits. We had to shout above the engine to make ourselves heard, and at the same time keep off the wasps that were shut in with us.

The driver had been a barman but had decided to work as a carrier because he didn't want to 'become a vegetable'. Of the twenty thousand inhabitants of Eboli, he told us, a third were loafers or people who lived off their wits. The remainder worked on and off or waited outside their doors for that precious envelope which contained a cheque from abroad, convertible into lire.

He also spoke quite dispassionately about a French girl he had met at Paestum. Her parents had treated him with amused condescension—lame and a foreigner into the bargain! This apparent indifference, which hid real bitterness and frustration, was an attitude we were often to come across.

The van looped and whirred up the burning road through scarred pepper-red mountains and across dry river beds. There was just a trickle of vitriolic water in one and, looking back down its broad valley, we could catch a last glimpse of the sea.

At a crossroads we clambered out beside the brown foaming river which flows from Pertosa grotto. The driver had to go on to Lagonegro. For a time we listened to the water, watching the dark eddies and the strings of bubbles gliding under a willow. Muddy, half-naked children splashed on the banks where women were drubbing their washing on flat stones. There was no village in sight, though the signpost bore the name 'Auletta', but the women told us that it was behind us, over the brow of the hill. 'You just climb up through the olive grove.' We did so in smoking heat over a dazzling chalk path and had to stop and rest half-way.

We looked back. The olive trees spread down and away, then up again to weave into feathery silver knots on the hills, tier after tier, placid and murmuring in the hot wind. A donkey ambled towards us, followed by an old man in corduroy trousers and a striped blue shirt which bore the stains of many dinners. The sight of two people carrying rucksacks brought back memories of the army. 'We had to go scaling mountains near Bolzano but, believe me, I've never had a pack on my back since then! We had as good a wind as the Northerners, mind, although they called us half-pints.' He looked at us shyly, as a young boy would, and shifted from one foot to the other, staring down at his nubbly boots which seemed to fit every bunion.

When he learned that we wanted to find an inn he guided us up to the village. The path led round a knoll and suddenly dropped into the main square beside the portico of the town hall, the one solid building which served to prop up the crumbling ochre and rose houses in the square. Down the main street we tramped, the old man smiling encouragement and mopping his brow. He stopped outside a low doorway and we followed him through a greasy bead curtain. When our eyes became accustomed to the darkness we saw a long narrow kitchen and flames licking in the heart of a stove.

The girl who received us spoke French. She worked in a factory in Paris most of the year and was only home on holiday. Though dressed in city style, there was something animal about her. She moved like a cat about the stove, thrusting in wood, springing to shake the frying-pan, but when she stood still her voice was quiet and compelling and she smiled only with her eyes.

The old man drank a glass of wine with us and then left us to struggle with a leathery steak which had been hastily prepared. The steak got the better of us, but we happily watched the antics of a fat puppy which poked its head through the holes in the cane-bottomed chairs and levered itself up the legs of the table to lick scraps.

I asked the girl, who was feeding her young man with soused herrings in the kitchen, if there was a room where we could rest. She led us to a bedroom—all indigo gloom—and pointed to a straw pallet on the floor. We settled down and were just dozing off, despite the swarms of flies and the grunts from the pig sty below the window, when the door burst open and our hostess asked if we wanted to meet her sisters and cousins. They had all come with their children, which had to be patted and admired while they sat and stared at us. But for all their show or friendliness, they grossly overcharged us when we left.

Word had gone round that there were strangers in the town and fat mothers holding their primped children hailed us from balconies as we passed. There were few men to be seen—they were working in the fields or had long gone abroad—but the policeman greeted us, a portly, slow-footed man in a green uniform worn almost white by sun and wind. They must have few law-breakers if so drowsy a man can deal with them.

In the back streets—steep tunnels of shade between the white houses—we picked our way through groups of women sitting on low chairs, chatting and sewing. One old woman, who was shelling beans, invited us to sit down, and we were soon surrounded by her neighbours, who vied with one another in entertaining us. They whispered and fled in and out of the houses. A liqueur bottle appeared for an instant but was found to be empty—blushes and laughter. Gradually their shyness wore off. They saw that we were simply glad to be there and so they offered us what they had—a few biscuits, and pears which they had brought from a field miles away.

The children climbed onto our knees; the women began to grin. These children were puny and silent; one had sores on his face and an empty gaze. A young mother, whose sleek hair was drawn into kiss-curls on her temples, was suckling a white wizened creature. We got ready to take a photograph—a mistake, for they all shot up to attention, clucking the children to them, and all hopes of a natural group were lost. The bean-sheller and her neighbour, a hawk-faced woman with gold teeth, smoothed their aprons over their sagging stomachs and stood as if thunderstruck, but the younger women grinned and bobbed, all except one who seemed ashamed to join in. I asked about her.

'Well, her husband went to Brazil two years ago and she hasn't heard a word since. She's afraid of people.'

A chorus of '*auguri*' and that gentle beckoning motion of the hand that means 'good-bye', a hint of regret in dark eyes, and we left their street.

Outside a manor house with its cool courtyard was a war-relic daubed in white: 'Sergeants' and officers' quarters'. The church roof blazed red against the mountains. The rusty hands on the town hall clock shuddered as it wheezed four. Donkeys, loaded with grain for the mill, shuffled in the shade. We turned our backs on the town. A gaunt man who had been pleased to stop for a minute and exchange a few words in Spanish stood gravely in the empty square, and waved and wished us well. And the wide square, filled with leaden sun, was like a silent arena waiting for something to happen in that world where nothing ever happens.

CHAPTER THREE

Lucania, Land of Light

THE road to Vietri swirls through scorched mountains and then climbs steeply for several miles to where the air strikes crisp even on the hottest day and there is the acid tang of broom.

A lorry picked us up an hour after we had left Auletta and took us to a hamlet beyond Vietri. The only shop was shuttered and silent. 'I doubt if they will open to-day,' said a man passing on his donkey, and muttered something about a patron saint.

The brassy light gave way to a pale windy sky and tossed clouds. The moors were shadowy, black and russet, filigreed with bleached grass. Nobody has tamed them. They spit up stones, crop after crop, and are never plough-weary. They brood round the shallow dips where the road winds—and the road gives you no easy pace. You are hustled forward to each ridge only to find the same lonely moors beyond. Though dark and deep there is no water in them—just a few soggy bog-bottoms where iris sparkle in the spring. For the rest of the year the earth sizzles and the south wind has a stony breath.

Part of this forlorn journey to Potenza was made with a mad couple in their little car. She was a fat Swiss girl who never got out when we stopped—mainly, I suspect, because we should have been hard put to it to push her rolls of flesh back into the car again without causing her irreparable damage. She spoke an amazing mixture of Swiss German and kitchen Italian to her boy-friend, a blank, nervous fellow who was obviously wondering how he could ever have fallen under her spell in the first place and—this was more urgent—how he could possibly get rid of her now. Their one diversion, an attempt to forget that they were together, was to screech and whoop at everyone we passed along the road. But then it must be hard to find scope for a riproaring holiday in the middle of Lucania.

It was dusk by the time we reached Potenza and we could see nowhere to put up the tent near the main road below the town. A barber who was leaning on the wall outside his shop came to our rescue. 'You don't need your tent. Come with me.' He showed us down some steps to a small house, once a café, which had been burnt out in a fight following a card-party and was being re-decorated. Here we could sleep, he told us, and we swept the floor clean of plaster and broken glass and settled down to eat our evening meal.

The walls of the room were puce and pear-green and the ceiling was all stuck over with old newspapers. As we fished sardines out of a tin, we tried to make out who had been the winner of the boxing-match between 'Il Diavolo Bianco' and 'Beppo il Bandito'. Another enthralling story concerned a wolf which had savaged sheep in a nearby village the previous winter, but the article ended abruptly at the most exciting point and we could not find the rest among the chequer-work of pages.

Children peered at us from next door through the trellis grown with passion flowers, but no one came to chat. The hills grew grey and cold and a flush of chill air came from the river where water glinted through red spongy turf. The horizon clicked up a notch; the sky swam with stars. The radio in the barber's shop was turned off and we fell asleep among the paint pots.

Painters woke us up early. While we were washing they gave each other rides round the yard in a wheelbarrow.

It is a long pull up to Potenza from the main road which bypasses the town. At a farm on the outskirts we stopped to buy milk. An old man, a trembling skeleton with transparent skin, made us sit on stools outside a filthy stall where the cows stamped to keep off clouds of flies. Ragged boys staged a mock battle for our benefit in the yard, clambering about on an antiquated horse-trap which squeaked and rocked, sending up spurts of dust from its ripped upholstery. After a long wait a tall, angular woman brought down two bowls of milk. 'We warmed it because . . . well, we always do it like that.' The sight of the stables made explanation unnecessary.

Potenza is the highest provincial centre in Italy after Bolzano. At first sight this seems unbelievable, but when you reach the crown of the hill on which the town stands, you are no longer surprised. There is infinite space and light, an ocean of hills falling away to the south and rising to the north where they gradually fade, range after range, into blue mist towards Venosa, the home of Horace. There is little left of the old town of Potenza. It was rebuilt after the war and is now a cluster of new houses, rose and pale blue, tiered like a wedding cake. People refer to it as '*la città*'.

No matter how early we got up, we always seemed to be too late to walk without the heat tiring us. The straps on the rucksacks cut into our shoulders and the sun beat down on our heads as we came down from Potenza and began to trudge towards Tricarico. The road flung out of Potenza and rose to the brow of a steep incline, over which it disappeared. To the south the river Basento, almost dry, curved in its valley below a patchwork of stubble and chocolate-brown earth.

A van stopped as we were resting by the roadside. The driver was a shy, fair-haired man with professorial spectacles. He was taking a sewing-machine to a house in Tricarico and offered us a lift. The first thing he told us was that he came from Taranto and he urged us to go there. 'It's a clean, civilised place, just right for tourists. What is there for you to see round here—*miseria, solamente miseria!*'

People in Mediterranean countries are very regional-minded. In Spain the wrangling between North and South is hard on the nerves. In Italy this attitude is perhaps more understandable, since the country has only been united for a century. The people in the South, through no fault of their own, know little of what goes on north of Naples—and, to Northerners, the South is an unknown land, vaguely disturbing and best left alone.

The van stopped outside a farm and the salesman gave a pip on the horn. A woman came striding down the slope and began to talk fast in the dialect. She was dressed in a long black skirt, blue blouse and boots. Her body was so bony and flat that you could have taken her for a man, and she held herself very erect and looked straight at you with her centreless black eyes. The conversation lasted some time, so we got out to stretch our legs. The valley below was silent in the sun, and as empty as a scraped egg-shell. There was only the hollow whisper of the earth pared to the kernel by sun and wind—a desert stillness in which you could feel the razor edge of each rock, the spur of each thorn.

The salesman hailed us and we set off. He explained that the woman had bought a sewing-machine on the instalment plan. She was unable to pay regularly—a family of nine living off that stony hill—so she came to talk to him every time he passed to reassure him that something would be done.

'She's a good woman,' he said, 'and in any case she needn't worry. Most people round here don't pay up. The machines just come back to us one by one.'

I couldn't tell whether the tone of regret was for the people or for the sewing-machines.

The road we were following was the Appian way, rolling over the high ridges to Brindisi. It turned south and entered the thick forest of Tricarico. We stopped to refresh ourselves at a spring of ice-cold water, the first I had seen since Auletta, and sat in the flickering shadow of oak trees where butterflies glided in the sun. This forest, which also contains stands of silver fir and beech, is wolf-haunted and wild boars grub its floor. Forests are rare in this arid region, which is equivalent in area to Kent and Sussex. The only other forest of any size is that of Accetura near Stigliano, which is forty miles away,

and all the superstitions and fears that have no breeding place in
the sun come to find refuge here—stories of werewolves, of
treasures buried by brigands, of gnomes and strange portents.

The trees rustled; the water sang. A cuckoo called, its voice
already broken by summer. None of us had any desire to talk,
still less any desire to go, but the sewing-machine could not await
delivery indefinitely.

Within half an hour we were in Tricarico, a huddle of houses
on a hump, some red or chalk blue, all dusty and eyeless. No
sooner had we got out of the van than a lanky customer reeled
out of a tavern and asked where we were going. 'To Matera?
You're mad!' he roared. 'On a hot day like this? On foot?'
But a peasant stepped along beside us and shouted back: 'They
can do what they like, can't they?'

He was very small, like a boy grown old in a night, and he
kept nipping in and out between us and feeling the weight of
our rucksacks to test the extent of our sufferings.

'I am going to Grassano, which is on your road. I know a
short cut. It only takes about three hours.'

We looked around us and realised that it was long past lunch
time and that Tricarico was already two miles behind us. We
had to go on.

Talk was of farming, though I wondered what any farmer
could get from such barren land. There are a few vines, poor,
crouching, sun-blasted plants, and corn which, on that unsuitable
soil, comes up as sparse as the hairs on a rat's tail. The trees
which once covered all these hills were cut down long ago.
The land dies every summer and in winter the rains wash it
churning to the sea.

The man asked us how much we earned and how we had
managed to come so far. Italian peasants think that if you travel
you must be very rich, but when they see you on foot they
cannot quite make it out. Perhaps you left your car somewhere
to see if you could walk a mile. The short cut was proving
long and gruelling. Our guide, who had nothing to carry,

ran ahead to a rise and waited while we negotiated patches of thorn.

'Let's sit down,' he suggested. His eyes roved over the stunted vines, then he said, wryly, 'The land doesn't produce much, it's true, but the women! If it gave fruit like our women, we should be rich. I bet you've no women in your country to compare with them!' He had seven children and no shoes to his feet.

The short cut had simply brought us round to a point further down the main road. We said we preferred to return to it in the hope of finding a car to take us towards Matera. Our companion looked crest-fallen but understood and we left him, still feeling the clasp of his rugged hands.

Half-way down the long incline we caught sight of a car bowling along the road in a cloud of dust. We reached the road just in time and the car stopped. There were four people in it already—a father, mother and two little daughters—as well as a great pile of luggage. We waved them on, but they refused to leave us there and, after much re-shuffling, we all squeezed in. They were from Bari and spoke a racy, tripping dialect. The girls spun out a rhyming jingle all the way to pass the time and squealed with laughter because we couldn't understand the words.

We passed Grassano and Grottole, silent skeleton towns, and descended the eastern flanks of the Bradano valley to Miglionico on its pinnacle of rock. Far away to the east we could see Montescaglioso in the flickering heat. All these towns ride like great ships, ochre and grey, on the waves of land, each clearly visible from the other. The road crossed the Bradano, empty as a sand-pit except for a few poplars, but far up the valley one winking eye of water remained in some sheltered ox-bow.

CHAPTER FOUR

Matera

As you climb up through the stony hills of the Gravina you see a line of modern cottages strung along a ridge. Can this be Matera? Surely there must be more to it than that. The people from Bari left us in the main street—low houses, dust-drifted pavements, broken masonry—and smiled at our surprise on finding that what looked like a heap of rubble was, in fact, the town—the modern town.

'Ah, Matera isn't so bad. It's a metropolis compared to the place where we are going—a little town near Altamura, empty, all the men have gone to work elsewhere.'

We walked until we came to a market place where there was a fountain. The water cleared our heads. We washed the visible parts of our anatomy and dried ourselves on our handkerchiefs, much to the amusement of a group of people who had gathered round to watch.

A gipsy boy pestered me to buy some peanuts. '*Kosko divus, pral,*' I said. He looked at me narrowly for a second or two and then beamed. I told him that we were gipsies, too, since we wandered about with bags on our backs and he laughed at that and insisted on shoving a handful of peanuts into my shirt pocket.

By this time it was well past two o'clock but, as the Italian sense of time is geological rather than solar, there were still restaurants open. We entered one, a huge cavern of a place, painted light blue. It was absolutely crammed but fairly cool. Sweating waiters hared in and out from the kitchen carrying pyramids of plates.

Above the wavering roar of voices you could still hear the angry whine of flies. Even in the innermost part of the darkest houses here the sun pries and burns.

After a wash and brush-up in the toilet which, apart from being flooded, possessed an unusual distinction in the form of a crucifix, we squeezed behind a corner table and found ourselves next to an engineer. He began to talk to us in French, pleasantly old-fashioned, such as you only hear in provincial towns in France nowadays. His opening gambit was some reminiscence about the Paris of the nineteen-twenties and the '*joie de vivre*' of Montparnasse; we hadn't the heart to shatter his dream by telling him that all that was forgotten, replaced by anger, mistrust and the harsh atmosphere of the police state.

He came from Catania and seemed very proud of it. Matera was his last government post before his retirement. He had spent much of his life in Greece, where his wife came from, and in Bulgaria. Though bitterly anti-government, anti-Catholic and well aware of the backwardness of the region in which he worked, he didn't seem to think he had any personal responsibility to try to improve matters. As he talked of misery and injustice in a closed world I thought there must be many like him in Southern Italy, educated and painfully clear-sighted. Even more than the peasants, who turn like blindfold horses on a threshing-floor, these people have reason to become aloof and resigned.

The engineer was insular, too, and what he might have done in Sicily he would never try to do in Lucania. Not that he lacked sympathy or understanding. He often burst out in impotent rage:

'And the clergy! Do you know that the monks and nuns who normally have no right to leave their convents are allowed out on election day because they are certain to vote for right-wing parties!'

No, it was no good doing anything, anyway—that is what he really thought—and he tried to stifle all his boiling grievances, hankering after the blue coast of Taormina, his own country, where he could end his days in complete forgetfulness.

The spaghetti had slithered down our throats long since when he finally rose to go. We sat on at the table, half dozing, while the old restaurant manager chevied a kitchen boy whose only sin was that he had red hair—no doubt an annoying rarity in those parts. The manager's dumpy wife kept plying us with bottles of mineral water and nodding encouragingly as we drank. She questioned us with the eternal formula which greets one everywhere in Italy, from men and women alike:

'Sposini?' 'No, sposati.' 'Fa molto?' 'Due anni.' 'Bambini?' 'Niente.' 'Ah, peccato! È Dio che l'ha voluto così!'

This interrogation, which in practice is much more prolonged, generally moves on to details of mothers, fathers and cousins twice removed. It is just a way of making conversation; any kind of answer satisfies. With the women, unfortunately, the conversation rarely goes any further and once you have described all the idiosyncrasies of your family there is little more to say. Italian women invest their total life's capital in their children. They are genuinely sorry and rather shocked to learn that you have none and probably think you are a sinner into the bargain.

From questions of progeny to those of religion is but one step, especially in Italy. The Church, of course, encourages large families—'increase and multiply'—and in doing so it not only swells the ranks of the faithful but lines its own pockets as well: children have to be paid for if they are to enter the fold. One of the disadvantages of birth control, from the point of view of the Church, is that it deprives them of a regular income at birth and baptism.

The wife of a sea-captain in Bari explained her failure to produce a large family (she had only one child) in this way:

'I know the modern methods for preventing child-birth and I use them, but I felt obliged to tell the priest about it. We arranged that I should make regular contributions to church funds to atone for my sin.'

Isolation and one-sided education have done their work in Southern Italy and the people, because the future seems to hold nothing, cling to the few strands of belief which are left to them. Sometimes, though, the fervent professions of religious faith that I heard sprang more from self-interest than from any other motive. Those who maintain that they are good Catholics do so because the village priest is the only person who takes any interest in their problems and because he does, in cases of dire necessity, give material help.

Those who look to the Communists do so because they think the Communists will provide a panacea for all their ills. So far the Communists have not been called upon to fulfil their promises, but they have at least organised centres in towns and villages where reading matter and film shows are provided and where discussion groups are held. Here people who have hitherto known nothing of what goes on outside their own village can learn how others live and can see that problems similar to their own are being faced elsewhere and resolved.

Feudalism is still the basis of life in Southern Italy. There is charity—a blob here, a dash there, all unevenly distributed—and the peasant receives a crumb so long as he remains true to those who hold the power—the landowners and the Church.

A village in Lucania

In the Sasso, Matera

CHAPTER FIVE

Matera—the Depths

THE upper town in Matera is called the 'Piano' and it is only when you begin to stumble down steep alleys that you realise that there is a lip of rock which marks the end of the modern town. Below this lip lies the Sasso Caveoso—old Matera. Here the limestone has been worn into an immense hollow riddled with cave dwellings hewn out of the soft stone. They are blinding white, windowless; black sockets serve as doors. It is as though, in a bad dream, you had come across a heap of skulls craning up from some huge charnel pit.

The Albaicin in Granada is gay in comparison with the Sasso for, despite the sun, the pit exudes hopelessness. The 'Piano' lords it above. The cathedral is on one edge of the bowl and grey administrative buildings on the other. Below them you feel trapped.

The sun exposes and emphasises the dirt and misery of Southern towns. The waterfront at Naples is as squalid and depressing on the brightest day as the quays of Liverpool are on the darkest. It is a question of contrast. As squalor under grey skies seems almost normal, we falsely imagine that all is gay where the sun shines.

The massive doors of the first houses we passed on the way down from the 'Piano' stood open, revealing leafy courtyards. Some women shelling almonds under a bower of wistaria looked up and smiled, but as we went on the houses became poorer. Pigs sprawled on the steps and there was milky, evil sewage oozing through the cobbles.

33

51920

A pack of children ran out from an alley and demanded
'una foto'—little boys who spat and little girls who bit their nails.
One small creature, who could not have been more than seven,
was very pert and self-assured. She asked where we had come
from.

'Oh, from France! Then I'll be Brigitte Bardot for the photo.'
And she began to pirouette, rolling her eyes and lifting her dress
(it was all she had on) to show a grimy, distended little stomach.
Her companions shrieked with glee. We laughed, too, for she
was a wonderful mimic, but I could not bear the expression in her
eyes. She had none of the serenity of a child and her voice
was husky. All the children seemed so fierce and confident,
more so than many adults—children to whom life never allowed
the luxury of being shy or innocent.

The alleys led down into the heart of the Sasso. For some
time we were followed by a group of girls and when we looked
round and smiled they ran to catch up with us. Flushed and
laughing, they smelt of cheap scent and sweat. They were
strong and supple and their smiles were bright water. They had
come from the country to watch a wedding at the drop-
shouldered church below us and invited us to accompany them.
Shy at first, they soon began to talk—especially one who was
working as a laundress. With her tender face, sleepy green
eyes and honey hair she was a figure from Botticelli.

For once we didn't get the usual 'family' questions. She was
interested to know if girls worked in England, how much they
earned and if they were able to study. Both her brothers were
in Argentina.

'And they will probably never come back. I should like to
go there,' she said. 'Taranto is the only big town I have seen.
My uncle took me there. He's a sailor, you see. Here we can
never go out alone—it's ever so dull.'

The other girls tittered. 'Oh, Franca, you are terrible!
What will they think of you?'

A girl who has her own opinion—what an idea! Yet she was

the head of the band and they obviously looked to her for guidance, with that mixture of awe and uneasiness in which a law-breaker is held. Her timid groping after something new and her half-admitted desire to leave home seemed revolutionary to the others. Resignation and patience have been the rule of these people for so long that silence, reserve, the gift of concealing what they really think have become second nature to them.

Franca spent all day on her feet in the village wash-house, with her hands in cold water, and for her day's work she earned four hundred lire—enough to buy one meal.

'Don't you go out at all, to cafés or to the cinema?' I asked.

'Oh, never to cafés; that's for men. We go to the cinema in Matera sometimes.' There was wild delight as they thought back over some scenes from '*Babette s'en va t'en guerre*'.

'And then there is television. One of our neighbours has television and we go to watch.'

Many houses have television but no running water. Films show parts of the world and ways of life only vaguely imagined before and there are special programmes designed to teach adults how to read. Hoary old peasants sit and watch these programmes every week. It is a fine and moving experiment but, while one admires the effort to make adults literate, it is curious to think that so many children are illiterate and liable to remain so.

The girls would not say which programmes they preferred. They saw that we knew nothing about the crooners they mentioned and were at a loss to say what else had particularly impressed them.

'Oh, yes. There is one thing. We have seen the Pope twice, the new one!'

I asked them if anything had been done to re-house the people in the Sasso.

'Well, the council offered to build flats outside the town but no one could afford to pay the rents.'

So there it is—'*buono per i turisti*', as someone said to me of

Naples; a 'characteristic corner' in guide-book parlance, though there are hardly any tourists.

It will be no easy matter to decide the fate of Matera. Of its 30,000 inhabitants, 18,000 live in the Sasso, of which there are two parts, Barisano and Caveoso. The dwellings, dug out of the tufa itself, are shared by men and animals. These men, who are mostly farm workers, go up to fifteen miles each day on foot or on their donkeys to reach the fields where they work; while many take the long road home every evening, many are also forced to lodge in the surrounding farms and return at rare intervals.

An attempt has been made to re-settle families in new villages outside the town, but relatively few have moved, for two reasons. First, they were unable to pay the rents, which amounted to 18,000 lire per month (a farm hand is lucky if he earns 900 lire a day), and, perhaps more important still, they felt lost, uprooted. The sense of 'togetherness' was gone.

In so poor a community there is strong feeling of neighbour-liness and solidarity which amounts to a kind of security. Help is always forthcoming when things are really bad. People depend on one another and are therefore willing to make a sacrifice in times of severe hardship. Once they have left their habitual environment they are forced to depend on strangers and on the authorities who, if they give help, give it in an impersonal way which cannot replace the simple heartfelt gesture of neighbours one has known since childhood.

The square in front of the church was shady. Priests scurried in and out of the side doors; a pyramid of tinsel and flaring candles shone through the velvet gloom inside. The girls joined the waiting throng to see the wedding.

Great dreams are woven into every square of embroidery worked in these lost towns by girls bent and silent in a doorway, their fingers worrying the rough canvas. They seem to be waiting for a handsome horseman to come round the wing of the hill and bear them off. As you go by you feel their furtive glance weighing up your masculine possibilities.

We left the girls to their wedding and climbed up on to the Piano again. In one back yard I saw two old women sitting, legs wide apart, on cane chairs. They were talking their heads off and one would lash out every now and then with a flabby rubber swat at the flies which swarmed about her. When she had fetched a fly down she just reached out slowly, never pausing in her chatter, picked it up, and added it to a neat row of black glutinous bodies on a stool in front of her.

The shops were re-opening. The Corso Umberto had cooled a little and loafers and the workless were drifting towards the entrance to the market. Something was going on. A close-packed, silent crowd stood gazing and listening—more than listening: they were drinking in the sound, gasping it in. Music is rare in the South and when it occurs it is not sweet or mellow but deep and hard, sometimes raucous.

The man responsible for the entertainment stood in the middle of the group. He was short and thick-set, dressed in a threadbare grey suit. His reddish face, lined and cracked like earth after a drought, never moved, but his eyes roamed up and up until you expected him to soar skywards. The wailing notes we had first heard had come from some old fret-saws stretched on pegs. These had now been laid aside and the musician began to play his cornet. The torrents in spring, the voice of the wind, the swelling choir in church, the buzz of flies, the sizzle of heat—all were in his music and it flowed over you until you forgot everything around you.

The men were choking with the music. I asked one old man who the musician was.

'He was once in a circus and now he travels the country, alone. We are all glad when he comes here.'

Time had come to make provision for our journey. We entered a shop filled with baths of olives—sepia and green pebbles, bright in brine. Huge sausages in their straitjackets

37

hung from the ceiling. The shopkeeper, a deferential little man, picked his way among the cheeses which strewed the floor and came to serve us.

'We don't see many tourists round here. Those who do come never speak Italian. Two weeks ago we had a coach-load —Dutch, I think they were—on their way to Greece. They just lifted their noses in the square, sniffed once and were off. You can't blame them, can you? Who would want to drag his carcass round here for long! Anyway, they came into my shop and had a fine old time prodding my cheeses.'

Greece made him think back to his soldiering days. 'We were up there in Macedonia. It's a lovely place all right, but the people were real terrors. We never dared go anywhere.' An eloquent gesture showed someone having his throat cut. I pictured the Italians in their natty uniforms, lost in the sullen hills near the Albanian frontier—the cream of Italy soured in an effort to subjugate their neighbours.

A vendor had displayed some pictures against a wall in the street leading out of the town. They all represented what people here aspire to—idyllic green landscapes such as few Lucanians have ever seen; snowy mountains, rippling forests, swans gliding on limpid lakes and courtiers sporting in mossy dells. The skies were violent blue, the snow plastery, the trees chubby and hideous in toad-green, the earth as red as bull's blood.

Matera is a disquieting place, stifling and shut in upon itself. From the south you climb to reach it but it never gives any sense of height or expanse. You reach the brow of the hill and are deceived. The town crumbles away beneath your feet. The misery of the Sasso is a blot which no other feature can redeem.

CHAPTER SIX

A Wanderer Returned

THE evening was all drowsy emptiness like the beginning of a long illness. A hoopoe called on the other side of the valley before the sun plunged into a cloud bank. Its call is the height of musical simplicity and, heard from afar, blends with this bare brown sea and the mathematical roads that trail across its surface.

The road faltered down into a dry hollow among sandy bluffs, all dovetailed and dropping away to the east. So like dunes were they that you would have thought the sea was near, yet it was twenty miles farther on.

There was a hovel by the road. A line of little grubby faces grinned at us over the fence.

'You want some water?' the children asked. 'We haven't got any. You'll have to go down there to the well.'

It was a domed white well, but there was a poisonous green smear inside the cowl. The battered bucket hardly fitted into the hole. The water glinted temptingly out of reach. It was no use trying, anyway, for there was no rope.

Someone was coming up behind us. It was a girl swinging along, quiet and self-possessed, arched like a bow. She had brought a rope and, as if showing children, she slowly tied it to the bucket and sent it down, breaking the scum on the surface. Our bottle was filled.

'There has been no rain for six months,' she said. 'Just look at that water!' It sat heavily in the bucket—yellow soup.

We told her where we had come from and she listened, unsmiling, though her eyes were sunny pools. A longing girl.

She stood silent, thoughtful, and then suddenly she flung out her arm. 'Go and see Giovanni. He lived in France and he'd be glad to see you.' Not half a mile away was another flat-roofed farm which before had merged with the dusty landscape but which now winked white against the mounting dusk.

The girl started to run back up the road, smiling for the first time and waving. The strain had gone; the strangers had been helped and she could go home content.

The farm stood in the middle of nowhere, without even a protecting tree, and the scoured earth had produced neither fruit nor vegetables. No dogs. Nothing moved inside the house, but doves cooed under the eaves and there was a whiff from the pig-sty and grumbling beneath the straw. Suddenly a sound of chopping came from a shed behind the house and an axe glinted blue in the doorway. It was laid aside and a man came out. He peered at us at first without saying a word, then brightened up when he saw our bags and dirty faces and came forward to welcome us. He was about thirty, tall and angular, and he had deep, kind eyes. His smile welled up from his whole body and flowered in his face.

We explained that we were on our way to the sea and that a girl had told us we must call on Giovanni. He chuckled to himself and, asking us to set down our bags, went into the house and returned with two rickety chairs. The chopped wood was placed in a raised brazier and flames were soon galloping along the olive branches and making glowing labyrinths of the thorn roots.

'The kitchen is no place to be in this weather,' he remarked. We had a thick soup of beans for supper to which was added the sausage we had bought in Matera.

Giovanni didn't ask many questions. He just watched us quietly and carried on as if our arrival out of the blue was quite normal. But I noticed that his hand trembled slightly when he poured out the soup and I knew that he was glad that we had come.

The fire died and the trailing smoke no longer afforded protection against the mosquitoes which bore down on us from every side, so we went into the house. Our host had been working in a tobacco field near the Bradano all day—a three-mile walk from the farm—and I think we kept him up beyond his usual hours and made the carbide lamp splutter longer than was its wont, but he wanted to talk.

He had realised very early that there was little for him in Lucania. Urged on by the example of other local boys, and against his mother's wishes, he had gone to Milan to look for work. 'They call us "the fellows with the wooden suit-cases" up there. Country bumpkins, they mean!'

At first he delivered newspapers. He slept in a hut at the back of the printing press and pedalled round all day in the stewing heat to shops and kiosks, dropping his bundles. 'I soon got sick of it and when the autumn came I decided to go to Paris. Milan seems so unfriendly to us, all business and hurry, and I thought I should be no worse off in France.'

In Paris he found work at the central markets unloading lorries. 'The money wasn't bad, but I lived in an awful hotel. The room was like a hole in the wall with one tiny window high up. On my day off I used to drag round the parks or along the Seine. I couldn't stay in that room. There were friends, all Italians, who invited me in, but most of them lived in one room in Belleville—you know those lanes with shacks and hordes of children—and there was always trouble with the "concierge" and trouble with the neighbours. I was taken for an Algerian several times, stopped and searched if I went back to the hotel late.

'Gradually I got to know some good French people, especially among the dustmen who lived in my street, and I'll always remember the way they used to laugh at me because I carried a leather bottle of wine wherever I went as if I was going to the fields for the day.'

Paris is a painfully aphrodisiac place to be alone in. There are girls, so many of them, but few to befriend a simple Lucanian peasant. Everyone seems to be in somebody else's arms; everybody seems to have a home except you. On chill Sundays you wander aimlessly and drift into any island of light and warmth, pretending that you are welcome in some seedy café full of giggling tarts where the manager snaps at you because you haven't given a sufficient tip.

Giovanni spent many such days. Too tired to take in the great whirling thought which is Paris, he was cabined in grey gulfs of streets, kicked like a football from one department of the Préfecture to another, badgered about working permits, threatened with expulsion by his landlady when, one night, he tried to get up to his hole in the wall with a Spanish maid.

'What I missed most was sun and open space. I put up with the rest all right.' For three years he held out and then, one day, a letter came from his uncle. There had been land improvements along the Bradano; a few homesteads had been built. Wouldn't he come back? He came back, knowing that nothing had really changed.

'I had hardly any money when I arrived because I used to send most of what I earned in France to the family. I bought this house with the help of a loan. It will take me years to pay it off and they only gave it to me because I am going to get married. She lives at Pomarico—a good solid girl.'

'Solid' probably meant she was ready for any kind of work— the next best thing to a dray-horse—but it was also the expression of a mind at rest: she would never stray far from home. Three years' glittering vision of female emancipation in France had not had much effect, yet Giovanni was a sensitive man with an innate respect for others. There was no swagger about him, no veneer. He just seemed happy to be himself again under the biting blue sky, and if his opinion of local life had been modified by his stay abroad (and it surely had, to make him so reflective) he had swallowed it into the darkest part of himself so that none should know.

These people do not change at heart. Even though they live abroad for years, fighting tooth and nail, they fall back into the old way of life on their return. A tarnished Eiffel tower, a calendar with coloured photographs of Paris and a few halting phrases of French—that was all that remained of Giovanni's three years in France.

The room was dirty and smelt stale. The table hummed with flies. No washing up was necessary for the cats had already licked out the pans. Giovanni was conscious of this but resigned to it. 'What can I do? I don't have time and anyway. . . .'

I asked Giovanni what he thought of living conditions in Lucania. He became quite heated. 'Why, they are bad, bad. Everybody knows they are bad. Here there is no water; the well is far away. But, one day, I'll have a tap; one day I'll make it a decent house.'

He stared at the floor for some minutes and then said, in a quieter voice: 'We could all do something to improve conditions but we don't stick together; that's our trouble. There was a lot of jealousy round about when I came back and bought this house, yet I have hardly any land and I work hard like all the rest.'

He noticed that we were looking round the room. 'I know what you're thinking. The place is no marvel now, but you ought to have seen it when I first came. You couldn't have seen it really because it was covered with briars, as thick as a mountain. An old man used to live here, alone. Half cracked he was and we village boys used to laugh at him. He had a wooden leg and he kept rabbits—hundreds of them in a pen. When he wanted to kill a rabbit for supper he would open the pen and the first one that ran out—"pum" with his leg. They finished him, those rabbits. One day he missed his aim and fell. He was found dying days later. Gangrene, they called it. We never call a doctor here. The old man stank; the house stank. It took me a year to make it habitable, what with the briars and the old vines that had bitten into the tiles. I lifted eight barrow-loads of sheep droppings out of the room where you are sitting now. You know, people here think animals thrive only if they live on top of us.'

The sheep droppings had gone but Giovanni still tolerated feathered company. A hen sat blinking on the end of a gigantic bed which stood ready, almost filling the room, to receive his bride. He offered us this, his only accommodation, but we refused to profane its quilted bosom and went out to sleep under the sky, lying on the rolling pebbles and vicious ridges of the 'garden'. We were to spend many such nights, though, as we travelled on, and the stones gradually seemed to lose some of their incisive quality. With time the body moulds itself to the ground, the limbs are rested and one awakes refreshed. In any case, in Mediterranean lands, one looks in vain for a grassy bed.

At cock-crow we were glad to get up, feeling like a sadhu just risen from his bed of nails, and prepare some tea against the morning.

Work was calling. Giovanni set off down the road towards the tobacco fields and we went with him. The land was flat, irrigated in places, and sown with maize—bearded heads nodding in the morning sun. A car came along the straight road and stopped under a eucalyptus tree. The driver knew Giovanni and offered to take us to the coast. Giovanni's eyes were full of confusion at our going. The grey eucalyptus leaves jingled dry in the sea wind.

CHAPTER SEVEN

Ionian Interlude

THE *Iliad* is the story of a fruitless struggle between peoples who can find no room for expansion. The *Odyssey* is an expression of the desire to explore distant lands, a tale of rivalry and jealousy on the seas in which the Phoenicians, represented as bandits, harass the Greeks in their wanderings.

It was a long, hazardous journey by the direct southern route from the Peleponnesus to Sicily, and so the Greek ships, to avoid Phoenician attacks, began to sail up the coast of Epirus and into the Adriatic. Corfu was founded in the eighth century B.C., then Apollonia in the bay of Volona and, finally, Epidamnus grew up on the headland above Durazzo. For nearly a hundred years the Greeks went no farther north into the Adriatic, but the current which flows southwards from Otranto bore their ships. They beached at what is now called Taranto, which became the first Greek colony on South Italian soil. From there a cluster of colonies spread out along the instep—Sybaris, Siris, Croton, Locri and, right at the toe, Rhegion.

The Greeks found a country very similar to their own as regards soil and climate—they called it Oenotria, wine country—but there was one important difference: Italy offered space. Nor had the Greeks to contend with an old established civilisation of the type they had found in Asia Minor and in Egypt. This gave them a free hand and a chance of expansion and enrichment such as they had never known before.

Greek civilisation in Southern Italy is the story of a growing taste for wealth and of megalomania which ended in disaster.

Taranto, the only serviceable port apart from Croton, became a town of some 50,000 inhabitants and a centre where muslin was dyed with the murex taken offshore. From the other towns came leather, perfumes and candied fruits but, above all, the whole of Greater Greece was a farmer's paradise. From one grain of corn a hundred sprang up, so runs the legend. The coins of Metapontum show an ear of corn; those of Sybaris, oxen; and slender, fiery horses of the Arab type figure on the coins from Sicily. Each town grew in splendour and riches. Contact with the local tribes was restricted to their enslavement. Lines of communication were opened up through the interior to the Tyrrhenian coast from Siris to Pyxos and from Sybaris to Laos over the Scalone Pass, this to ensure the flow of goods from Ionia to the other Greek colonies in Etruria.

Sybaris was queen of all the cities. Some authors maintain that there were as many as 300,000 people living there and that it was enclosed by a seven-mile wall. Sybaris was the emporium for goods coming from Miletus and its citizens wore opulent himatia made of wool from Asia Minor. Pottery was manufactured on a large scale for the export of wine and oil, and there was even an underground wine pipe-line running to the embarkation point at the mouth of the Crati.

The Greeks of Magna Graecia were not imbued with tradition. They possessed initiative and a keen business instinct, but power and wealth gradually went to their heads. Along these spacious shores they built, in their desire to impress, temples four times larger than any in the Greek homeland. The golden cloud of luxury which hung over the whole coast eventually began to create rivalries. Active, pugnacious even, as these cities were, they began to tread on each other's toes. Encroachments occurred, quarrels arose. Arbitrary actions on the part of tyrants led to implacable strife, unparalleled in the Greek world, and finally, like the cannoning of so many billiard balls, one town bowled the other over, devoured it, and, carried by its own impetus, moved on to rend its neighbour. Sybaris destroyed

Siris and, in its turn, was wiped out by Croton which fell to Locri in the fifth century B.C.

Plato once compared the Greek colonies on Mediterranean shores to frogs round the edge of a pond. The Italian frogs burst through being too proud. Magna Graecia today presents a sorry contrast with the glory of past times. It must have been rich indeed to support cities of such magnificence as Sybaris. The earth wore a different coat then. The forests were almost untouched, the rivers full-flowing; good husbandry was the rule. Whole cities were provided with water where drought conditions now prevail for three-quarters of the year. Deforestation and neglect have all but ruined a fruitful land.

The Temple of Pythagoras—the Italian name, le Tavole de' Paladini, is a relic of the wars with the Saracens—is all that remains of what was once the Greek city of Metapontum. Whether Pythagoras really settled here and formed his school is still open to conjecture; that he died here seems certain.

In ancient times the sea was only a mile from the present site of the town and there was a harbour. Excavations are still being carried out in the direction of the sea and a huge necropolis has been found. The temple columns rise sheer and are visible for miles; yet, when you reach them, you find they are sturdy bulging pillars of soapy golden stone and the impression of grandeur gained from a distance melts into one of intimacy. The pillars glow, calm, benign, and shepherd you in among them.

Metaponto stands near the main road from Taranto to the south, but the rumble of lorries does not disturb its peace. The setting is pastoral. Sheep browse close to the temple. The fields round about it are planted with tomatoes and tobacco and there are white and rose farmsteads within sight. Trees laden with peaches curtsey in the hollows; green fields drift away towards the misty line of the sea.

The small museum at Metaponto certainly repays a visit. It

contains some beautiful vases, jewellery and bas-reliefs as well as some excellent maps which help to situate the old city. A gay little building in shining stone, it had only been open a few weeks when we got there. The attendant, a bear-like man decked out in what looked like an admiral's uniform, padded round after us with a duster tightly clenched in his fist, ready to pounce on any finger mark and keeping a weather eye open in case we scrawled anything unseemly on the immaculate walls.

We finished looking at the treasures and decided we needed a wash; we had found no water that morning. Up till then the attendant had been willing to tolerate us as would-be searchers after knowledge, but he was discomfited by our request for water, the more so as there wasn't any. It appeared that the museum had not yet been provided with the usual offices. The attendant wrinkled his nose and drummed his hairy fingers on the piles of postcards. Finally he marched us out through the back door and pointed to where, in a field, some lusty young women were thwacking washing in an emerald-green bath. This was more than enough for us but he still looked perplexed. As we went through the house, I noticed that, though there really was no water, the rooms were tastefully furnished, tiled throughout and sparkling with copper-ware.

Twenty years ago the region of Metaponto was a desolate stretch of sand and marsh where hardly anything was cultivated. The peasants kept horses and goats; the big landowners neglected their estates and were loath even to gather the scanty crop of olives and almonds each year. Now there are fruit trees of all kinds, including oranges and lemons, and tobacco has produced excellent crops.

This is one region where the *Cassa per il Mezzogiorno*—the organisation which provides economic aid for the South—has made a real effort to improve conditions. Peasants living in the barren mountains inland were invited to settle in the plain. Many responded, but there has been trouble in persuading them to abandon small plots of land, which generally did not belong

Making cheese

Our tent in a clearing—Sila forest

to them, in favour of better land near the coast. Debts and expropriations have always been their lot and they mistrust the authorities.

Peach trees afforded the only shade during the afternoon and a resting place that night. A tin of sardines and a piece of bread that would have been better suited to the rockery than to the supper table was all we had to eat, but peaches and tomatoes made a welcome dessert. Some peasants gave us a whole basketful. They had been working in the tobacco fields all day. There was a pretty matronly woman, her husband who came forward shyly and couldn't decide whether to take a cigarette or not, and a lanky boy who was wearing a cap about three sizes too big for him and antiquated ankle boots which resembled fungus that had sprouted buttons.

Their daughter, a girl of nine who already possessed a measured, womanly dignity, kept pushing away a tot who wanted to romp with us. She stood stock-still, trying not to stare, and then suddenly dashed away in search of something else to give us— the peaches were too commonplace. Back she came in a little while and solemnly presented us with a single corn-flower. I gave her a five-franc piece. She examined it closely and then asked if she could buy anything with it. When told that it was only a keepsake she handed it back without a word. Her grown-up airs came to an abrupt end when the tot at last succeeded in putting a handful of earth down her dress and they went off into the dusk, rolling and somersaulting like cubs.

The peasants had warned us about mosquitoes. We came out of the all-night struggle haggard and longing for a bathe. A tangle of briars, sporrans of vetch, dry swishing reeds—that was the path to the sea. The viscid green trickle of water in the Bradano gave way to patches of cracking mud where dragon-flies veered and hovered. The sirocco was blowing, clammy and stifling. The long muscles of water came plying in, rippling to crash in a bath of foam. The higher waves strode in behind, tossing their heads in plumes of spindrift.

The beach was deserted except for a goat with amber eyes, nibbling at thistles. The sand was strewn with sea lees—splayed starfish, crunch-dry crabs, horned eggs of dog-fish, splintered wood bleached silver. Here and there, in pebbly cradles where the waves had sucked, trembled clumps of pink sea-thrift. There were no gulls, only a turnstone busy where the waves scalloped the sand, revealing a harvest of sand-hoppers.

We found some sand-lilies. They, like the oleanders, are among the few flowers that defy the drought. Their slender white throats, lightly coated with grains of yellow, are cool reminders of spring—a season one tends to forget on this dry coast. There were armies of ants to watch, too, and lizards which came close to challenge us before scuttling away into a crevice. When peach stones were thrown to them they stared, puzzled, for a few seconds and then pounced on them, worrying them as a dog worries a rat.

A day soon passed on that beach. The smothering sound of the sea dispelled all sense of time.

CHAPTER EIGHT

Nova Siri

THE region through which we had been travelling is generally known as Lucania, though the old province of Lucania, slightly larger than it is today, extended beyond the two provinces of Potenza and Matera. These provinces are sometimes referred to as Basilicata, the name given to them in the eleventh century when they were ruled by a Byzantine administrator, a 'Basilikos'.

The largest rivers in Lucania, the Bradano and the Basento, are now used for irrigation and it is thanks to this that the plain of Metaponto is fruitful. The rest of the Ionian coast, except for the oasis of Sibari at the mouth of the Crati, is arid. In Calabria it is totally barren, and from the Gulf of Squillace to Cape Spartivento water is as scarce as in the desert.

One day I picked up a local newspaper and the headline *La popolazione sofre la sete* caught my eye. In a small town in the province of Reggio people literally had no water to drink. For two years the local authorities had been promising that within a few days water would be gushing from every fountain. There was, in fact, only one fountain, from which water did not even drip, let alone gush. The tone of the article was one of weary desperation. Every year the same appeal goes out in many parts of the South, and every year the response is the same—an empty promise.

Aqueducts are being constructed, but work is slow and irregular. It is estimated that 69 per cent of the towns and villages in the South have insufficient supplies of water. There are adequate reserves in the Calabrian Sila, but the villages on the coasts, which are no more than forty miles away, go thirsty throughout the summer. This problem of water was forcibly brought home to us when we reached Nova Siri, the southern-most coastal village in Lucania. We arrived perched on a lorry carrying sugar-beet—a significant cargo because sugar-beet, as the driver told us with evident pride, is a crop completely new in the region. It was a mile from the main road to the sea and a joy to be on our feet again after the sickening jolts and choking smoke-screen of the lorry.

Beyond the sleeping station, through which the mud-brown train from Taranto to Reggio rumbles twice a day, was what had once been a restaurant. If there had ever been any affluent visitors there were certainly none now; the shutters were rotting off their hinges and the garden was a jungle. Opposite was a low-built trattoria. A group of men lay sprawling in the shade outside.

'This way for a good meal!' they chorused, smiling and waving.

The village postman was among them, nursing the handful of letters that had come in on the morning train. There he would spend his time dozing or chatting until the sun had moved a respectable distance down the sky, enabling him to deliver the mail in the first cool of the evening.

It is difficult to look spruce and smell sweet if you have no water. There was no water in this inn and no lavatory in most of the houses in the village. In Lucania 67 per cent of the houses have no lavatories, as opposed to 15 per cent in the North. No one wishes to deny people the right to relieve themselves in the open air—the wind surging behind you makes you feel very earthy—but that this procedure is hardly recommendable in towns is shown by the high percentage of typhoid cases in the South.*

---

* In 1962, 146 deaths were caused by typhoid in Italy. Of these 91 were registered in 'Il Mezzogiorno', where the highest figures were as follows: Puglia—43; Campania—20; Basilicata—7.

Though the endemic bucket serves as a lavatory, it is sometimes replaced nowadays by a porcelain throne, but the run-away system seldom bears examination—a stagnant pool at the bottom of some garden gives ample warning of what to expect.

We left the inn in the full heat of the afternoon. An iced coffee revived us before we set off for the beach. Neapolitan coffee is a pitchy syrup laced with ice and so strong that you could trot a mouse on it.

On either side of the road to the sea oleanders and tamarisk had been planted to bind the sand, and there had been some attempt to make the land fit for grazing. In one field, covered with patches of yellow grass, cows stood restless and fly-maddened under a reed shelter. A stocky figure was leaning on the gate and gazing ecstatically at the cows.

'*Vanno a mangiare pronto,*' he said in a dropping, cajoling tone, as if talking about children.

He was a roadmender and one of those rare souls with a fund of innocence and good nature that poverty has not managed to undermine. A stone, a butterfly, a cloud would call for his attention and he would stop and smile a sudden child-like smile that showed fine, regular teeth. His eyes, wrinkled with crow's feet, would flash, urging you to share his joy.

We were chatting to him in the shade of a hump-backed bridge when we heard someone coming along the road: it was the roadmender's companion. He, too, was short but very dark and, unlike his friend, appeared wiry, purposeful.

'Do you mind if we go with you to the beach?' they asked. '*Un po' di riposo*! Work can wait!' The situation demanded a sacrifice and, in any case, the road would still be there when they came back. They pitched their bags under the bridge and, flanking us, stepped out briskly so as not to lose a moment of their free afternoon.

This Italian gift for throwing everything up and taking life easily is inimitable. I suggested, much to the amusement of the roadmenders, that they adopt 'Shirkers of the world, unite!'

as their motto, but they reminded me that, by South Italian standards, even to be a roadmender is the height of fortune; it is a regular job and paid by the state.

There were few people on the beach but those few, as is always the case in Italy, were lumped together in one place with miles of empty beach on either side. Ladies were supposed to undress in a tent, so L was whisked away by an elephantine matron in a dirty dressing-gown which yawned at the wrong places.

The fine grey sand was almost too hot to touch. The sirocco was puffing hard and shovelling in packs of oily clouds which banked up over the rocks that dribble seawards from the heart of Monte Pollino.

While we undressed, the second roadmender fumbled furiously with his thread-bare uniform and finally appeared dressed only in some coarse woolly underpants that would have kept out the worst winter chill. He went off into the water with two other men who had joined our group, and they sported round a floating log which they had succeeded in dislodging from the sand. His companion did not venture into the water but shouted instructions and warnings.

'Keep inshore! Don't get out of your depth!'

There was no cause for alarm—the beach shelved gently down and one had to wade far before the water came up even to one's knees.

The log escaped, nosing off into the waves, and the revellers returned to dry themselves on the beach. A young man, fox-featured, took a special interest in us. He had finished his studies at a school in Potenza and was lazing away the holidays on the beach, waiting to go to university in the city of his dreams, Naples. We coaxed him into speaking French, but he hovered timidly on the brink of every word and was thankful to relapse into the polished Italian he put on for our benefit.

Suddenly there were some sharp exchanges between the student and the roadmenders. The student was defending government policy, but came in for some fierce criticism from Rocco, who was a thoroughgoing Communist. Silvano, who hated political discussions, dodged about behind his friend, throwing in a word now and then and trying to restore calm.

The student praised the work of the Cassa per il Mezzogiorno. 'You have seen the hoardings advertising their work, haven't you?' he asked, turning to us. We had no time to reply.

'Hoardings! I should think they have. Plenty of them!' shouted Rocco. 'And does that prove anything is being done? Not on your life! Why, all the land round here still belongs to one man, a count. Do you call that fair dealing?'

The argument ended abruptly in laughter because the road-menders saw some people from their own village way off along the beach and cast about for a place to hide their caps, so that they would not be recognised and branded as slackers. I teased them for not sticking to their principles.

CHAPTER NINE

Inland again

We decided to cover a few more miles before nightfall. The student stayed to take another dip, but the roadmenders helped us on with our bags and came to see us off. When we reached the main road they stood apart a moment, whispering. At last Rocco asked if we would go with them to their village near Rotondella. 'There is a bus at six o'clock but if you come we'll walk to keep you company.

It was impossible to refuse such an invitation and we set off down a terrible pot-holed road in the direction of the hills. As we trudged along I asked Rocco what the argument on the beach had really been about. He maintained that, despite government propaganda, nothing of real value had been done to improve conditions for people. Though he admitted that the dam on the Sinni and the irrigation scheme in the plain of Metaponto had improved farming, there was one thing he could not get over—the lack of drinking water in the villages.

I mentioned the new homesteads built by the Cassa per il Mezzogiorno near the mouth of the Sinni.

'Yes, I know, but only the richer peasants can afford to buy those.' Payment is long term but beyond the means of the vast majority, the *braccianti*, who continue to work for a few rich families owning immense tracts of land. Our Communist declared that most of the credits assigned to the Cassa went into the pockets of the officials anyway. Occasional visits to the local Communist party centre had influenced him considerably. He refused to go to church and had only one child.

'How could I bring up a large family on my wages?' he said.

Silvano took no part in politics and never voted. This he explained rather unconvincingly by saying, 'Whatever we do the government will still do as it likes.' He probably did not know it (and would not have been much concerned) but, under Italian law, nobody can have a passport unless he can prove he has voted.

Rocco could read, slowly and following with one finger, and he told me that his grandfather, a man of over seventy, had been to the *Scuola Populare* and had learned to read and write there. The Scuola Populare for adults had great success during the first years of its life, but of late attendances have dropped. Now they have begun programmes for the Scuola on television, and people gather in a friend's home, or at the priest's house, to watch and learn.

About a quarter of the people in Lucania are illiterate; and there are some who have forgotten how to read and write. There is an acute lack of schools and the children start to work so early that they seldom attend school regularly. Some say they could study at home—but one look at the average house in any Lucanian village is enough to tell you that no child could study properly in such conditions.

The village was not far off, crouching between the last claws of the hills where they dug into the plain. Above it stood yellow cliffs scored by the wind, and to the north, across the valley, the hills heaved up again, hiding the valley of the Sinni on the other side. The eye tired of the unrelieved yellow clay, ridge upon ridge of it, crust-hard. There is little that is green. Only here in the village were a few umbrella pines that made a shady spot near the cemetery; fig-trees pushed their elbows through its ruined wall.

The sun was just setting. Troops of men and women were returning from the fields, some straggling in twos and threes, others waxing and waning in one long line, all converging on the village. A kerchief fluttered; a hand waved across the stubble. They walked very erect, mostly in silence, but smiled as they passed and then suddenly turned when they realised that we were strangers. The men had greasy caps, torn trousers, shirt collars turned up and great ungainly boots. The women wore full-length skirts and walked barefoot.

Tired and footsore though we were, it soon became very apparent that we could not stay with the roadmenders. In these villages the rough stone houses, which look like piles of rubble, generally have only one room, sometimes two, into which the whole family is herded. The windows are very small and the rooms very dark. Rocco lived in such a house. When his wife showed us into their only room it took some time to get used to the gloom. There was a smell of mildew, of something sweet and sticky, a whiff of wood smoke and urine.

A bed creaked and we saw a little white-faced girl who stretched out her hand to us. A decrepit grandmother mumbled incoherent things from her chair near the stove and snapped her dry-stick fingers, the nearest she could get to a show of excitement.

Silvano went off to the room he rented over the one *vini cucina* in the village, and I went with him to buy something to eat. I found some spaghetti and a hunk of cheese, but there was neither olives nor fruit to be had anywhere. Luckily we had some grapes left over from the previous day, and, on returning to the house, I asked our hostess to give them to the child.

'No, she never eats grapes. They make her ill.' The offer of fruit was, in any case, superfluous—the village gardens were strewn with rotting figs which no one had troubled to pick up.

There is so little besides pasta. Potatoes and chestnuts are given to the pigs which produce excellent pork on such princely fare. Vegetables are very rare: lettuce is unknown, and the tomatoes, seldom eaten fresh, are dried on boards. The treacly, pip-sprinkled mass which becomes golden in the sun is used as sauce—for pasta, of course. There are plenty of almonds but they are mostly exported, and the chestnut trees which grow wild everywhere in the mountains have a low yield because they are never grafted.

One striking thing about the Ionian coast is that there are no fishermen, so the peasant's diet is never cheered up even by a sardine or a sea-bream. This part of the Mediterranean is poor in plankton and too deep for trawling.

In Rocco's room we sat on stools round a trestle table to eat the frugal supper. The hunk of cheese provided amusement for all. It turned out to be a mansion inhabited by lively maggots which popped out onto the table, looping the loop and shimmying their fat, wrinkled bodies with considerable mastery.

'Our cheese always has maggots,' said Rocco. 'Don't let them put you off.'

'But what do you do with them?' I asked.

'We close our eyes and eat.'

The roadmender spoke measuredly, seriously, and his wife, who gazed intently at us with her frightened eyes, kept crossing and recrossing her hands. She had finished with the cooking pots and now sat bolt upright, her breast heaving, her dress clinging to her flanks, darkened with sweat and fusty with earth. When her husband spoke she added weight to his words with a series of long, slow nods. The little girl babbled so fast in the dialect that I understood nothing. I felt as a doctor must feel at a consultation. The wife was both awed and relieved by the presence of someone to whom they could talk freely, a complete outsider who would not blab or scoff.

They told me about their daughter. She had suddenly fallen ill and was partly paralysed. There was only one doctor within a radius of twenty miles and he had refused to come at first because he thought he would not be paid. He did come eventually, after repeated assurances that he would get his fee, and said that the girl must be sent to hospital. A collection was organised in the village to pay for the ambulance and the child was taken to the nearest hospital, at Taranto, sixty miles away.* She was unable to stay there long because the treatment had to be paid for in advance and, even with help from Communist party funds, the father could not meet the cost himself. All that had happened three months before and there the child lay, fretting all day, improving little.

Rocco's family typifies the way Lucanian peasants live. Half the people in South Italy live more than two to a room. The state health service exists in name, but it is so hedged about with forms and certificates that simple people give up in despair, daunted by the system of payment in advance and subsequent reimbursement.

The roadmender's room looked as if it had been furnished with pickings from a flood disaster. The floor was spattered with chicken droppings; scurf from combs clung round the feet of the chairs; the handles of unwashed pans protruded from under the bed. The nearest fountain was two hundred yards away in the village, and there you had to wait your turn before you could fill your jar at the trickle from the spout in the wall.

In South Italy the houses are dingy and depressing. In Greece and Southern Spain they at least look bright, though those who live in them can hardly be said to be rich. I asked many people about this reluctance of the South Italian to create even a minimum of cleanliness and comfort. The reply, with hands outstretched and eyes uplifted, was, invariably, '*a che cosa serve?*'—what's the use?

We were too tired to put up the tent. The roadmender's wife lent us some sacks to soften the bumps a little, and we found a level resting place near the cemetery wall. Our host said good-bye to us, for he had to be up before dawn, and we watched his stocky figure disappear in the moonlight.

---

* In 1962 there were 1.3 hospital beds per thousand inhabitants in Calabria and 2.1 in Basilicata as against 9.5 in Venezia Giulia and 8.5 in Liguria, two of the Northern provinces.

CHAPTER TEN

Dolce Vita

I REMEMBER once seeing a woman in Naples who wanted to hire a cab. The driver was dozing on his box in the afternoon heat and he refused to take her. She pleaded, she threatened, but it was all of no avail. He just gave her a withering look, closed his eyes and returned to his thoughts, while the old skeleton of a horse snuffled loudly in its nosebag.

'Is he paralysed? Doesn't he want to earn an honest lire?' she shrieked. I sympathised with her, but I also felt sorry for the driver. No matter how much he earned, he would never have enough to make ends meet. We spoil life by wearing ourselves out to provide for its continuance—that was his philosophy.

It is incidents like this which convince foreigners and people from North Italy that the South Italian is good-for-nothing; and certainly, in the towns, the number of idlers and café loungers lend support to this impression. The matter is not so simple, however. Italy has become a house in which a large family, poverty-stricken, occupies the ground floor, while a more prosperous family lives in comparative ease upstairs. Why is this?

The South is obviously not favoured climatically and is over-populated—but over-population is a fairly recent phenomenon which is as much the result as the cause of poor economic conditions. Italians have always attributed the glaring contrast between North and South to historical factors. In the North, freeholdings were not uncommon even when Rome held sway.

The feudal system was not so severe as in the South, nor did it last much beyond the twelfth century, for the influence of the towns brought peasant slavery to an end. Feudalism sank its roots into the South when the North was already sloughing it off. In the South it has remained the basis of social life up to the present day. It is no exaggeration to say that, since the disappearance of the Greek colonies, the people of Southern Italy have lived on the border of survival because of the oppression and incompetence of the ruling classes.

The picturesque indolence of the South is the result of history and of a climate which alternately shrivels and inebriates. A refusal to be hurried is an enviable quality, yet these people possess little else—it puts a healing plaster on their frustration. But they are not all people who enjoy an aimless, empty life for its own sake. Anyone who has seen the South Italian peasant at work knows that he is neither lazy nor incapable. Men and women alike are out from dawn to dusk, waging a ceaseless war to win something eatable from a land so poor that it is not fit to support half the present population. They work like beasts of burden and when, at the end of the day, they lift their faces from the earth, you wonder that they are human beings at all.

The attitude of that Neapolitan cab-driver is understandable. People are loath to work when there is no incentive. The years spin out, empty and unrelieved. Sons migrate; a trickle of money comes in; and one jogs on, tired of fighting for a toe-hold in a society which resolutely refuses to provide the barest living. Years of privation have contributed to creating the atmosphere of stagnation which broods in the South.

Cold figures, though they can give no inkling of individual hardship, do help to clarify some of the problems which South Italy has to face.

The total resident population of the Mezzogiorno in 1964 was a little under nineteen million, with a labour force of 6,244,000. In 1959 there were half a million unemployed in the South and just over 600,000 in the Centre and North. This number has since diminished, partly because of national industrialisation projects and land improvement aimed at providing more work, but largely owing to steady emigration over the past five years. In 1964, however, there were still 206,000 unemployed in the South, compared to 343,000 in the Centre and North with a population of 33,263,000 and a correspondingly larger labour force—13,886,000. (These official figures only concern *registered* unemployed and take no account of the vast number of under-employed.)

In 1963 277,611 people left Italy to seek work elsewhere and, of these, 207,078 came from the South. The emigrants go to other European countries, to the U.S.A., Australia and South America. There is also an estimated seasonal migration of Southerners to Northern Italy of 60–70,000 each year. Emigration is encouraged in the hope that it will relieve over-crowding, but its effect is cancelled out by the extremely high birth-rate. Most of the emigrants come from the towns, which means that potential talent is being drained away from the areas where it is most needed. Of the factory managers and civil servants born in the South, 54 per cent live in the North, while only 3.5 per cent of those born in the North have moved South.

What of educated men like the engineer we met in Matera, who have seen both worlds and felt the gulf that divides them? Too often their attitude is that of a person who is gravely ill. His being dissolves and he sinks into himself, watching, some-times with morbid interest, the progressive deterioration of his strength and faculties. He yearns to act, but all action seems futile. It is interesting, in this connexion, to see how Italian writers have reacted to the problems facing their country. Some, like Carducci, attempted to create a national literature of an optimistic kind, but this movement was not followed up, for want of any intellectual rallying point. In the latter half of the nineteenth century only two writers exposed, realistically, the miseries of peasant life—Giovanni Verga in Sicily and Grazia Deledda in Sardinia.

63

Croce was the most influential thinker of the century and many consider him to be the most outstanding personality of modern Italy. He was a humanist who distrusted myths, whether political or religious, but his attitude—resignation in face of unreason—was strongly coloured by his Southern background.

In Pirandello one finds the same intensely personal and, at the same time, local view of life. Though he became internationally famous, he was acutely conscious of being a Sicilian as well as an Italian and a European. *Liolà*, one of his finest plays, was written in the Sicilian dialect.

After 1945 Italy turned over a new leaf, both economically and intellectually. In fact, over the past twenty years, Italy is unique in having produced a literature which aims at developing a whole social consciousness. One might almost call it an experiment in literary sociology. It is a literature of social protest, comparable with Victorian literature in intent and scope, though not in form and content. It is also regional, a natural consequence of the uneasy unification of North and South which took place only a century ago. In Italy, at least, all roads, and especially cultural ones, do not lead to Rome. As any traveller realises, linguistic unity is by no means complete. For Southern country people Italian is a language which is learnt at school and which has not developed of a piece with their way of thinking.

Since the war a host of writers, most of them left-wing, have dealt with specific aspects of life in certain regions. Vittorini describes the poor in Sicily; Scotellano writes of the *contadini* in Calabria. The life of the working classes in Florence is the theme of Pratolini's novels, while Moravia's work is a fierce satire on the Roman middle class.

The greatest revelation has been the condition of the South, which we owe, principally, to Elio Vittorini (*Conversations in Sicily*, 1941) and to Carlo Levi, whose unique account of life in a small Lucanian village (*Christ Stopped at Eboli*, 1945) gives some hope for the future and makes concrete proposals for helping the peasants to improve their lot.

Ironically enough, it was because certain intellectuals from the North—Cesare Pavese was another—were exiled in the South by the Fascists that people in the rest of Italy began to learn about parts of their own country which had always seemed as remote as the moon. Ignazio Silone had written of his native Abruzzi in the thirties but he, too, was an exile abroad at the time.

The one exception to this 'engaged' literature is Giuseppe di Lampedusa whose novel, *The Leopard*, was written from an aristocratic standpoint. Yet it provided a picture of the very conditions which gave rise to the stagnation and injustice so often attacked by left-wing writers. In exploding national myths he expressed the pessimism which many Italians feel. He saw life as a constant alternation between struggle and acceptance, but his conclusion was that all resistance is bound to fail.

The other important element in this more than Dickensian effort to promote a national sense of responsibility, and one which affects a far wider public, is of course the cinema. This industry since the war has been closely linked with the literary movement: many talented writers have devoted themselves to writing film scenarios. In the 1940's a series of films appeared which presented daily life in a way calculated to stir the conscience—an experiment in disillusion. Most of them dealt with personal tragedies caused by war and unemployment; De Sica's *Bicycle Thieves* and *Sciuscià* emphasised the effect of poverty on children. These films, which tended to be blatantly sentimental, were at once Italian in atmosphere and universal in application. They were effective both as a shock to bourgeois complacency and as a mirror reflecting to the working classes their own condition. After a showing of *Umberto D* hundreds of pensioners demonstrated in front of the Municipio in Rome.

It was not until 1947 that the social implications of poverty in the South were explored on the screen. Visconti's *La Terra*

Trema is a Marxist version of a theme taken from Verga: where Verga blames fate for proletarian misery and exploitation, Visconti accuses capitalism. A more recent film by Visconti, *Rocco and his Brothers*, 1960, illustrates the impact of Northern industrial society on Southern immigrants, showing how some of them fail to integrate because their wholly foreign code of values is misunderstood.

In 1961 De Seta produced *Banditi a Orgosolo* which is both a documentary and a film-poem in its own right. It captures the spirit of Sardinian society, the natural balance of which is destroyed by blind, authoritarian interference. *Banditi a Orgosolo* seems to be more effective than the more realistic films as a comprehensive study of a society and its physical environment —perhaps because it is allowed to permeate the mind instead of being forced upon it.

Part Two

CHAPTER ELEVEN

Our Brothers in the South

THE road which enters Calabria from the plain of Nova Siri is pushed gradually closer to the sea by cliffs, until, at Montegiordano, road and railway line seem to be jockeying for position at the edge of the waves. Beyond Amendolara the red cliffs are gashed by dry river beds, ovens of simmering light which reveal shadowy peaks far to the north—the mountains of Dolcedorme, cool and Arcadian from a distance.

It took us nearly a day, with a lot of walking and one lift, to get from Nova Siri to Trebisacce, a dead town of one narrow street where groups of boys circled maddeningly on their bicycles, yelling and cursing whenever they escaped being run over by a passing lorry. A young man from Turin on his way to Sicily took us as far as Sibari and there we decided to stop for the night. There was one shop, a garage and some railway sidings where brown engines chugged up and down like maybugs or sat steaming and sighing together. Nothing else stirred in the great plain which spreads south to where the Sila forest looms above Rossano.

The river Crati loses itself in the marshy plain and crawls sluggishly into the sea through a network of ditches and thick banks of reed that divide fields of tobacco and lucerne. The hot wind, the runnels of water and tangled vegetation make the atmosphere so oppressive that you feel incapable of effort. No wonder the Greek colony of Sybaris was renowned for inhabitants who idled their time away in luxury.

The people in the shop stared at us in amazement when we

said we were going to stay the night. 'There is no hotel. You must go on to Spezzano Albanese.'

We began to look for flat ground to put up the tent but found only ridges, reed beds or water. After trying an orchard where a giant dog threatened to chew our shins to the bone, we wandered out of the village and came across a big white building with *Ufficio Agricolo* written over the main gate. This seemed to offer our only chance and, in the gathering dusk, we hurried into the courtyard to put the hospitality of government officials to the test.

At first we could see nobody. The tractors and harrows had been put away; the squealing of pigs proclaimed that it was feeding time. Eventually an old man carrying a bucket came out from behind the stables and we asked him if he could help us find a place to spend the night. He scratched his close-cropped head and said, after some reflection, that there were plenty of spare rooms where we could spend the night out of the way of mosquitoes, but that we would have to wait to see the manager, who was expected shortly, in order to ask his permission. He suggested that we could wait in the caretaker's lodge. There an old woman was looking after a baby which in no time succeeded in wetting my trousers and opening all the pockets in the rucksacks. The old woman, spindly and parchment-faced, with a lock of pure white hair peeping out from under her blue kerchief, chattered like a jackdaw. She spoke so fast and in such an astonishing dialect that I missed most of what she said and just hoped I was making the appropriate replies. I did gather, anyway, that she had four sons in America and two in North Italy. It was impossible to keep count of the daughters.

This prolific relic assured us that children were the only things worth any consideration in this world. But she added, with a doleful expression, 'they abandon you in the end and it's hard to get used to that.'

The old man, who was some distant relative, spoke more

intelligibly. He told us that the woman lived alone in San Giorgio in the Sila Greca and that she was Albanian. This Albanian colony is centred in the Sila Greca but has offshoots all over Northern Calabria. The Albanians came to Italy in the fifteenth century to escape the Turks after the defeat of their national hero, Skanderbeg. In the Sila they found wild mountains and forests similar to those they had left behind them and founded a group of villages which now bear Byzantine names like Santa Sofia d'Epiro, San Demetrio. They have retained their language to some extent, though the young people prefer to speak Italian. These people belonged to the Greek Orthodox religion, but they have been forcibly Catholicised over the years. One can still see the *Popa* in his stove-pipe hat in some villages, especially in the Piana degli Albanesi, the other large Albanian colony south of Palermo.

The old woman took a liking to us. She closed all the windows to keep the mosquitoes out and, leaving us to be eaten by the contingent already in the room, she busied herself preparing cups of coffee.

'I do hope you will be able to stay,' she said. 'There is room, but with that man one never knows.'

As we were sipping our coffee a car drove into the yard. The woman looked startled and, touching us both on the head by way of benediction, she stole away into another part of the house. The cause of her anxiety soon appeared, short and stout, bustling out of the car with a great show of displeasure. He demanded to know who had brought us there and, in the same breath, assured us that we would get no place to sleep. There was no preamble, no *buona sera*. He then strutted outside the gate, beckoning to us to follow him, and pointed to the sign. '*Ufficio!*' he roared. '*Ufficio! Non capisce?*'

I informed him that I was quite capable of reading the name and added that we had no intention of disgracing government property with our presence any longer. At this he saw he had gone too far and suddenly became fawning and conciliatory.

'I shall take you to a place where you can put up your tent,' he suggested. There was nothing for it but to accept as, by this time, it was quite dark and the moon had not risen. During the short drive up the coast hardly a word was said. As I had expected, our benefactor took us to a horrible place which he thought ideal. There were pines, it is true, and fewer mosquitoes, but there was also a gaudy hotel—the first of its kind we had seen since leaving Salerno—rows of bathing huts, glaring arc-lights and a juke-box.

A few couples still shuffled round the cement dance-floor—there were two German girls in the languorous embrace of local beaux—but most of the people were sitting in noisy groups under the trees or fluttering like starlings before settling down to roost.

The chief tried to make polite conversation before leaving us. The first thing he told us, very proudly, was that he was from Bologna. 'I am an agricultural engineer. They sent me down here two years ago to live among these savages. I often come to this hotel; it's the only place where one can have a bit of fun.' Undaunted by our silence, he went on:

'We from the North, we are like you, used to a civilised atmosphere. They are a foxy lot, these people, you will see. Never trust them. We are spending millions to improve their conditions and a lot of thanks we get for our trouble!'

I replied that it was high time something was done.

'Yes, but you don't really understand. These people have always been used to bad living conditions. They don't appreciate anything better!' He, by the way, ordered mineral water when we went to the bar. 'The tap water is undrinkable,' he said, looking slightly embarrassed. Not undrinkable for the locals is what he meant.

It is not surprising that, in the South, the overbearing Northerner who prides himself on being 'civilised' is resented. This man could hardly have set a worse example to those whom he considered beneath him and, riding rough-shod over them as he did, I am sure they retaliated by ensuring a minimum of co-operation.

The South is notorious for its lack of trade unions. The workers are unable, or unwilling, to form groups, and all that unites them is their common bitterness and the daily scramble for survival. An old man said to me one day, 'We pull the rope. We pull and pull, day after day, but in the end it breaks.' When the rope breaks it means that a man opposes authority and becomes an outlaw.

CHAPTER TWELVE

Storm over the Crati

EARLY next morning a tremor shook the pine wood. An earthquake, perhaps? No. The rumbling, chuckling noise ceased abruptly, to be followed by the patter of hundreds of little feet, eddies of laughter and the clap of hands. Within half an hour the lido was a boiling mass of children. They had come for the day from Senise and Morano. The buses which had brought them lumbered off behind the hotel. I could hear the drivers discussing ways of filling in time. They decided on a swim followed by a good binge, and one of them suggested the German girls might be ready and willing.

Washing was the problem of the morning. The taps in the hotel had given up the ghost completely and the pump outside needed attention.

By eight o'clock the first grown-ups began to arrive—mothers getting into voice for the day's foray, with curly-headed tots in tow; fathers edging away from the family, waiting for a chance to seek refuge at the bar with their cronies; young couples, bouncy and alert, dashing to the beach where they could feast on each other, with their eyes at least.

We drank coffee on the hotel terrace. The German girls came out to have breakfast and the bus drivers lost no time in introducing themselves and settling round their table. Foreign girls, being rare south of Naples even in season, are assured of unremitting attention. The men I talked to who had been lucky enough to hook one were generally dissatisfied. The ease of their conquests took the tang out of it all, for one thing, but their chief complaint was that the girls had no 'stomach', as they called it.

'They never really give themselves,' one man said. 'You feel they are bored and you're as good as anybody else, just to pass the time. Now our girls are different. They wear you to a frazzle, they drive you mad, but they become part of you.'

Centuries of religious badgering only serve to bring out pagan qualities. Realistic in every sense, these people have no time for donkey love and are baffled by our wishy-washy, conscience-stricken type of affection. People pretend to be shocked by the unabashed animality of the Southerner, but the Italian sees its differently. To him a refusal to admit what one feels and to enter wholly into what one does is ' ugly '. And this aesthetic appraisal, as opposed to a moral one, is used for something which fails to satisfy all the senses—something unbalanced, incomplete, dishonest. You seldom hear a Greek or an Italian justifying himself in these matters. He is honest enough to act according to his lights.

The pump had been mended and water was now spurting out of it, uncontrolled. It was brackish, hot and cloudy, but the jet was taken by storm. People splashed through the filthy pond underneath to fill their bottles and wash grapes. Everybody was sweating hard in the still, sultry air. Several children were stung by wasps that clung round the water pipe and the water itself brought no relief, for those who drank it felt stickier and hotter than before. We waited until there was a slight lull and then dived in under the pump, but no sooner had we begun soaping our faces than a forest of cups was held up between us and the water. Nobody asked us to go: they just stared at us, unblinking, while the thirsty crowd thickened and pressed closer.

L tried to talk to some of the girls in charge of the children to find out how the outings were organised, but they volunteered no information and stamped off towards the beach, shrilling at the children to keep them in line.

We had been taken, against our will, to the lido because most Italians think all foreigners are bound to want to go to this kind of place. At least they have the merit of being avoidable, since they are clearly marked on most maps.

It was a four-mile walk back to Sibari past fields where girandoles flung rainbow jets of water in the sun. We were resting at the cross-road near the station when a small car drew up and two young men, their straw hats tipped back at a rakish angle, asked where we wanted to go.

'Cosenza? Get in and welcome!'

The road ran near the river Crati, bubbling creamy yellow. There were poplars along its banks and oleanders wind-blown on the bare islands in mid-stream. Almost at once the driver began to sound us out on our political views. What had we seen? What did we think of the work done by the Cassa per il Mezzogiorno? It turned out that both men were leading lights in the Communist party centre at Cosenza. Once they had got memories of the Moscow youth festival off their chests they began to talk about their own work, and assured me that the province of Cosenza was full of Communists and that the Albanian communities were red to a man—perhaps a sentimental link with Enver Hoxha.

I asked what their programme was. The answer was rather vague: 'We have centres in most villages, and discussion groups, and there is usually a library. You will notice that the Communist peasants are much better informed than the others.'

'Don't you get a lot of opposition from the church?'

'Of course we do, and we are fighting hard against it, but it's a tough job. You see, people here don't like change. No matter what we say to them, about 80 per cent of our supporters insist on getting married in church and on having their children baptised. They believe in having a foot in both camps!'

The landscape was changing as we sped along. The plain with its melon patches and knotted tracery of stream-beds gave way to hills at Terranova and between the hills were dry, grassy bowls set round with dwarf oak and pine. Flowers appeared, suddenly familiar: purple rest-harrow and yellow vetch struggling out from the burnt grass and rocks. The wind blew stronger. Smoke-yellow clouds thickened over the Sila; great ships of shadow floated on the mountains. The road was suddenly filled with whipping dust-spouts.

'Let's stop for a drink and sit out the storm,' said the driver. 'It won't last long.'

The inn was a tumble-down place and right next to it was a gipsy camp—a few shelters made of reeds under which women and children crouched. I always noticed that the gipsies are not despised here. People help them whenever they can. When all are poor, no distinctions are made.

The rain came. At first it only spattered the dust, but soon it began to boil in a white frenzy on the road. The palm tree outside the inn thrashed in the wind. Over a glass of wine the two men began to talk about the land reform and its application in the province.

'Of course, to the outsider everything looks fine along the coastal plain,' said the dark man who was the more talkative of the two. 'You see new farms and fields of tobacco and you naturally conclude that the region is prosperous, but you don't know what really goes on. The government has taken land from the barons—and there are plenty of them round here—but only the poorest land which was always lying fallow to provide them with hunting reserves. The peasants have to work doubly hard to rid that land of stones and make it cultivable. In any case there wasn't enough of it to go round.

'When the law for the distribution of land was finally voted there were thousands of people on the lists but only a few hundred have received their share.'

'Not only that,' added his companion, 'the big landowners have been very clever. They appear generous but, behind the scenes, they bribe, falsify papers and lie. They will do anything to avoid giving up the good land. Along the Coscile, for example, there is one baron who still owns four thousand hectares. The government hasn't dared to dispossess him because it is said that he cultivates the land well. Everywhere the barons have kept the vineyards and the olive groves and those, of course, are what bring in the money.'

'What about the co-operative farms?' I asked. 'Have they had any success?'

'Oh, there was a plan to create some but the whole thing fell through. Now even the farmers who have land find it difficult to sell their produce. The trouble is that the farms are far from any village; transport is difficult and of little use, anyway, as there are no distribution centres.'

The plains of Sibari, Sant'Eufemia and Metaponto are the only regions where farming could be done on a sufficiently large scale to warrant collectivisation. The government has preferred to distribute the expropriated land among a few peasants who develop a kind of family autarky on a small, unproductive plot. The situation resembles that which faced the Communist governments in Eastern Europe just after the war. The land was at first parcelled out in such small lots that very low productivity resulted and, to remedy this, they had to create collective farms.

I was interested to know how the peasants reacted to the sudden possibility of having their own land.

'Well, they have been used to being exploited and in debt for so long that many of them didn't want to take a farm or just wouldn't believe that it really belonged to them. They reasoned like this—"We have always been in debt. Before it was the barons and now it will be the state. We shall simply exchange one bad master for another!"'

The rain had stopped and was lifting from the hills. The heart of the storm was moving away northwards.

'The first rain for three months,' said the driver. 'We need a climatic reform as well as an agricultural one!'

We went out to the car and set off along the road to Cosenza.

On the dashboard I noticed two medallions, one a Virgin and the other a St. Christopher—strange possessions for a rabid Communist. I doubt if any Italian car does not contain some such medallion, usually accompanied by the photograph of a sad-eyed mother or a pale girl described as 'my sister'. Beneath this panoply appear stock injunctions—'Drive carefully. Think of those at home', or 'Your loved ones pray for you'.

Since the reform began in 1950, over 130,000 families have received land; but the problem is that, even if all the land were distributed equally, there still would not be enough to provide a reasonable standard of living for each family, owing to the tremendous yearly increase in the birth-rate. The immediate aim of the reform was to provide work for as many people as possible. In this it has been successful, but there is no guarantee that, in the long run, the expropriated land will be exploited so as to give the best results.

The Communists, according to the two men, would forcibly reduce all private property to about a hundred acres. 'But here everybody thinks of his own interests first. We can only convince those who are already convinced—the adepts. Many trail along behind us, hoping to benefit from anything we do, but hangers-on are just dead weight. As to the others, the enemies, we shall have to use compulsion and make them swallow some grit. No more lording it!'

They saw me smiling.

'Ah, you may smile! You don't know how lucky you are with your traditions and all the rest of it. Your slow democratic methods will never work here.'

CHAPTER THIRTEEN

Cosenza

IT was late when we arrived at Cosenza. The streets, still glistening from the rain, were empty. The Communists recommended a restaurant and took leave of us in their business-like way, entrusting us to the care of a waiter who was one of their disciples. He placed us near a table round which were gathered cadaverous gentlemen with hair plastered carefully over their bald patches. They sat stiffly, as if their corsets were too tight, and were having a hard time refereeing the chatter of their spouses, wattle-necked gossips whose yellow, blotchy hands were gauded with rings like carbuncles.

A daughter like a goddess, cool in pale blue, sat silent and wide-eyed, her curves accentuated by the studied tilt of her head, her slim legs folded demurely sideways so as to leave no doubt about their trimness. She bathed in the glow of male stares; the waiter stared so much that he came near to letting a plate of soup dribble down the neck of one of the ladies.

Peasant girls smoulder. They are silent, proud, as straight and pure as an iris, seldom coquettish. In polite society girls are different. Under their langour and 'baby doll' prettiness there is an almost virile perseverance devoted unswervingly to one aim, that of getting a husband.

Engagements last long, five or six years sometimes, for the suitor has no chance of marrying until he has proved himself reliable, hard-working, and, if possible, ambitious. The engagement begins tentatively. There is polite talk in the drawing-room, some frantic whisperings in the kitchen—the maids are

Cecita—an upland lake in the Sila

Calabrian peasant women—Tiriolo

used as go-betweens—followed by evenings at the cinema, the fiancée being always accompanied by sisters or friends. Before marriage the man often has to finish his studies and obtain a job, and in Italy this is a very long process. Meanwhile the girl waits—a miracle of continence—until the great day. Lucretia is the example that she must follow; her chastity must never be questioned. She knows that he frequents prostitutes, but she accepts it as something normal. It affords proof of his masculine capabilities and is a reassuring sign that he has no intention of forming other more permanent liaisons. If he sows his wild oats, she reasons, he will probably appreciate her the more once they do eventually get to bed.

That, of course, is the whole trouble. After so many years of purely formal relations, spiced only with a little flirting, marriage in its early stages turns out to be a dismal failure. On finding that they are really strangers to each other, the couple become stale, depressed, inordinately jealous. The wife is set to work to produce children; the husband escapes from home as often as he can. Passion, contrary to what films and operas would have us believe, is rare, and is usually the expression of a desire to dominate where no other form of self-assertion is possible.

What Robert Burton wrote of Italian love-life in the seventeenth century still holds good, to some extent, today: 'The Italians lock up their women and will not suffer them to be near men. But we are very far from such strange conceits, and will permit our wives and daughters to go to the tavern with a friend, and suspect nothing, to kiss coming and going, which they cannot endure.'

As in Spain, sexual repression is very evident. The rich Italians who return from Paris loaded with photograph albums of nudes have become a standing joke. I remember seeing a young Italian just married who was proudly showing his libidinous purchases to his astonished bride. In Italy one never sees lovers kissing in the streets or parks. A heavy fine awaits those who demonstrate their affection in public. To shield people from licence, the church has established censorship of films, television programmes and plays. Lists of films considered unfit for public consumption appear in the newspapers and those which are banned usually contain some harmless bedroom scene, while gangster films which show people being beaten to death are passed on to the public without comment.

A little man was sitting opposite us. He, too, had been staring at the group at the next table. 'They are lawyers,' he said. 'Cosenza is full of them.'

He kept shaking his head, fidgeting and clacking his tongue as though displeased with the world. He showered salt and pepper on the food as if trying to kill the germs. Having passed me a magazine to occupy me while he ate, he turned his attention to a fish which positively bristled with bones—one of those formidable Mediterranean specimens. The struggle was Homeric but the fish came out on top and he applied himself gratefully to an easier prey, a downy peach.

'Where are you from?' he asked, munching noisily. 'From England! From so far! You have a car, of course.'

He was thunderstruck when he learned that we were travelling on foot or at the sweet will of the populace. 'I expect you are going to the Sila. You must take the *trenino*. You'll never be able to walk all the way up there. I am going there today for my holidays, but I take the *trenino*.'

The presence of two foolhardy wanderers put him off his stroke completely. He bobbed and fidgeted more than ever in alarm. ' How can you travel about like that? It's dangerous. There are queer customers on the roads, you know. Only a few weeks ago an American boy was injured not far from here. He was travelling with a girl and some men tried to molest her. When he defended her they knifed him and tied him to a tree. Terrible business.'

I never discovered whether the story was true or not. South Italians take delight in telling hair-raising yarns to frighten people. It is a part of their natural gift for histrionics and also, perhaps, of a desire to enliven their own boredom from time to time with a juicy story, real or imaginary. Personal grievances are settled by murder, that no one will deny, but vengeance is a local matter. That foreigners should be attacked seems to me to be out of the run of things and, more likely than not, a question of mistaken identity. We never travelled in great style and could hardly be taken for wealthy visitors. Those who tour by car, loaded like Christmas trees with paraphernalia, are an easy target for malefactors, and the stories of spectacular robberies in Italy are too well known to need repetition.

I found that our lunch-time companion had never been farther than Reggio, though he was a professional surveyor. Among the Italian middle-class people are afraid of travelling, afraid of change and accidents. Their heads are still full of stories about brigands. The peasants, on the whole, were especially surprised to find we had no car, but they did not think it strange to roam as they themselves are often forced to turn their backs on the only land they know and seek a livelihood abroad.

The afternoon was more than half-way through by the time we escaped the surveyor and his dark warnings and were able to go and explore Cosenza. The new town in the valley, which has grown rapidly since the war, is aggressively modern. The Corso Mazzini resembles the main street of some American boom town and contains buildings which try hard to be skyscrapers. *Standa* is one of these—the Italian equivalent of Woolworth's—and a wonderfully clean, well-stocked store it is. There one is served by charming examples of Calabrian girlhood in blue smocks. They come as a surprise because women here rarely work in shops or offices. In Lucania they help their husbands in the fields, but in Calabria their work is confined exclusively to the home.

The jostling crowd of shoppers stared at us and at least ten different people asked where we were from. Some pretty plates caught L's eye, were duly purchased and packed up. As they would not go into our rucksacks they had to be sent by post. At the post office we were given reams of forms to fill in and the sallow official behind the counter told us that the parcel was insufficiently packed.

'And you had better register it, too. Half the parcels here disappear.' But he added, considerately, ' Oh, it's not really worth the trouble. Why pay more when the parcel will probably be stolen anyway?'

The nearby shops had no gummed paper so, reluctantly, he condescended to cut strips of brown paper which he proceeded to stick on the parcel with watery post-office glue. As he stamped the forms the strips peeled off, slowly but surely, rolling up with a final snap, and when he turned to grab the parcel they webbed and lingered round his hands. We disgraced ourselves by laughing and, in a fit of desperation, he flung the parcel into the trolley behind him, saying it would have to risk the journey packed as it was. We never saw the plates in one piece again.

Cosenza, surrounded by mountains, is stifling in summer. The sticky heat had closed in again an hour after the storm had rumbled away. An ice-cream barrow outside a cinema offered temporary relief. Passers-by gaped and goggled. How they stare in Cosenza! Just as the glistening blobs began to drip on to the pavement a young man came up to us.

'Why eat your ice-creams in the street?' he said. 'Come across to my house.' There were his father and mother beckoning to us. They opened the half door and we passed from the dazzling street into a cool room that smelt of new-washed stone and lavendered linen.

The mother prepared coffee and brought out a plate of dried figs, walnut-crusted and baked in the form of a cross, which are a Calabrian speciality. The son talked of the week-ends he spent fishing in the Sila and pointed out the interesting spots on the map. The technicalities of fly-fishing strained my Italian, so the old father came to my rescue. He was a quiet man with a bad squint which gave him a pitiful, beseeching look. Casting about for something to entertain us, he hit upon an album full of faded photographs. Groans from the family.

'You have seen them all umpteen times, but to some they are new!' he chided. He flipped the pages, trying not to appear too excited. There were wattle huts in Somaliland; himself in spruce white ducks standing near a thorn bush in the middle of a stony waste; a gala evening in the garden of some hideous Government House. Colonial days. A sword glinted on the beams above our heads. The old man smilingly refused to give any explanations.

The son coaxed his sister, a shy, doe-like creature who was on the point of leaving school, to show her prowess in French, but she would not be persuaded and stared desperately into her coffee cup while her mother laughed indulgently.

When we had given a thumb-nail sketch of our lives they began to talk about Calabria and were eager to hear our impressions. The father brought out a Communist party membership card, a blazing star on a green ground, so there would be no doubts about his sympathies. I told him that two Communists had brought us to Cosenza. He smiled broadly.

'You will meet plenty more of us, don't worry! Perhaps you don't know, but the government had to hurry up with the reform in the Sila because they knew local opinion had reached boiling point. Promises and still more promises, that is all they ever gave us, and then there was that incident at Melissa. What happened there? Well, the peasants lost patience and began to occupy the land belonging to the barons. The *carabinieri* were called. They lay in wait and fired on the peasants as they were going home. Several were killed. It was a near thing for the authorities; in Calabria killing is repaid by killing. If they had not started to distribute the land there and then the whole province would have been up in arms.'

He was a retired assistant engineer living on a modest pension;

the son had a thriving ironmonger's shop and a motor-tricycle and the daughter was studying at the *liceo* in Cosenza. The mother steered the conversation round to less fiery topics and everything ended in laughter when she thrust a packet of dried figs into my rucksack for the journey.

The waters of the Busento were red and foaming that evening after the rain. We crossed a bridge and, passing through a covered market, furnace-hot, came out onto the road that leads to the Sila. The road climbed steeply on a level with the castle, the cathedral and the Academy which rise above a jostle of red roofs, the old town.

In the last shopping street we took a photograph of two nuns—the tall and the short of it. They looked down at the pavement when they saw the camera and then, just as they passed us, raised their eyes which burned with scorn and resentment. This little scene amused a potter who was sitting outside his shop. He gave me his address and asked me to send him the snap. 'I'll pin it on the wall in my shop to cheer me up!'

He asked for all the details of our trip and sighed regretfully at the thought that he had never taken to the road in his youth. 'I once went to Naples in 1920. That is the farthest I have ever been and for me it was a real adventure. To think that there are so many people who would like to travel! No chance of moving now. I'm stuck here selling pots, and few of them at that.'

The pots were restful to the eye: rose, dusty green, pumice grey. There were some round which rings of girls and boys danced, green, vermilion and black on a white ground. 'Those come from a special school here,' he said. 'I only make the ordinary *bamboli.*'

He raised his hat to a group of old men who had come to sit on a bench on the other side of the road.

'Look at them. That's it; take a good look. Now you can

say you have seen some of the oldest inhabitants of Cosenza—
our honoured citizens! Most of them have never had a regular
job in their lives. There were no jobs, unless you went to
America. There they sit, waiting to die, just hanging on,
thanks to some measly pension. You are young. Life is on
your side. I have been listening to fine speeches for fifty years
and I haven't heard a sound bit of common sense yet. You
might be luckier.'

Disillusion and regret, that beating undertone of Italian life,
can become obsessive and depressing. Each complaint, each
jibe, each grudge swells into a river of voices in one's mind.
The surface foam, which hides the despair beneath, is made of
brittle laughter. These people are never gay. Toughness and
astuteness save them in the face of overwhelming difficulties.

We had been walking for an hour when a man stopped and
offered to take us as far as Spezzano della Sila. He was an
engineer, a suave fellow with cold green eyes and a sombre
Byzantine face, and he spoke what sounded like Chicago-
Calabrese, the result of six years spent in America. He left us
in the village and we walked on, looking for a place to pitch the
tent. The slopes on every side were sheer and the few terrace
fields were narrow and covered with hard clods.

As we scrambled down a path the earth crumbled, our bags
dragged us down and we landed, in a shower of stones and
dust, on a ledge where a few olive trees had managed to obtain
a root-hold. There was just room for the tent.

The sky turned apple-green, then violet, and finally burned
in a long orange flame over the mountains westwards, and the
darkness swarmed up from the Crati valley. The air became
cool. Somewhere below, frogs began their age-old laughter.
A pebble rolled. Silence. Mice scuffling in the stubble.

CHAPTER FOURTEEN

Stone and Pine

THE Sila—the name comes from the Latin *Silva*—deserves a short historical sketch.

There are, in fact, three Silas in Calabria: the Sila Greca in the north, where the Albanian villages are; the Sila Grande in the centre, between lakes Cecita and Arvo; and the Sila Piccola round Lake Ampollino. This region, once inhabited by the Bruttians, was well known to the Greeks. They used the pines from the forest to construct their fleets, and so did the Romans after them. During the Norman domination it became the property of feudal barons and to this day almost the whole forest is privately owned.

For many centuries the Saracens raided the coasts of Calabria and, to escape the double curse of piracy and malaria, the people living near the sea began to move up into the Sila, where they cut down trees and cleared land to plant their crops. This deforestation, and the planting of crops unsuited to the soil, has turned the Ionian shore into a lunar waste—bone dry in summer, devastated by the torrents in spring which eat down into the clay and leave deep bare ravines, the *calanchi*, a typical feature of the Ionian landscape. The destruction worked by ungoverned water is completed by the wind which blows away the top soil.

Until very recently the Sila was a wasteland, a hunting reserve for the nobility. If people went there at all it was to cut down more trees indiscriminately, though the barons rented some land and summer pastures from one year to another to peasants who paid in kind. The population of the Sila was nomadic and engaged only in seasonal work. There were hardly any villages or means of communication and no organised cultivation. Potatoes were planted one year, rye the next, and the land was then left lying fallow for two years. Of the estimated 191,000 acres of forest, only half was exploited at all.

Since the war roads have been built and villages have sprung up, but the latifundia have hardly been touched and only fallow land has been taken over for the agrarian reform. It is amazing that the Sila, which is so rich, should have been neglected so long. The soil is capable of producing excellent corn, potatoes and forage crops and recent experiments give promise of high yields in sugar-beet, flax and sunflower seed. There is also unlimited scope for market gardening because, when the season for vegetables comes to an end on the coast, it is only just beginning in the Sila, 3000 feet higher up; there is no lack of peas, beans and strawberries even in August and September.

It was dawn when we woke in the field near Spezzano della Sila. Someone was walking round the tent and whispering. I looked out and was greeted by a labourer and his wife who had come up from their shack on the hillside to see who we were.

'We thought you might be bandits,' they said, half joking, half serious.

'Where can I find water?' I asked.

The man led me to the end of the field past a muddy pond where a pig wallowed. 'That's not the water,' he said. 'It's higher up.'

After a lot of scrambling we reached a spring, the first I had seen since we had passed through Tricarico. It ran thinly because of the long drought but it was icy cold. We both dashed water on our faces and laughed like children.

'*Acqua buona, aria buona*,' he said. That is the first thing the peasants in the Sila tell you about their forest. They have good reason to be proud, for few places in Calabria can boast either of good air or of good water.

There are no villages on the road between Spezzano della Sila and the uplands thirty miles away. A green leprechaun of a roadman shook his head at us as we passed.

'You won't get up there today at that rate!'

There was no hurry and walking was made pleasant by the shade of chestnut trees. Two miles back there had only been olive and almond trees and now there were chestnuts with ferns growing beneath them. A little farther up there was another spring, strong-gushing this time, its spout choked with bubbles.

The road swung in a hairpin bend and began to edge round a deep valley before rising towards the col which leads to the Sila itself. We were resting on the parapet of a belvedere when an old rattle-trap of a car bounced round the bend. Two men got out and came to admire the view.

'Do you want to go up to Camigliatello?' they asked.

We did. In a quarter of an hour we had reached the col of Monte Scuro where there is a television station, and from there we had the first view of the great tableland of the Sila.

To top the ridge below Monte Scuro on a hot summer's day is both a surprise and a relief. It is like leaving a steaming bath to plunge into snow. The valley below is a trough of sticky heat and then suddenly you emerge where all is clear and crystal. The pine forest drops away to Lake Cecita, side-steps the lake and storms the low hills that rise in the distance, blue and hazy. The wind has an edge on it. It tumbles the hissing pines, then dies away, and in the lull that follows the sun strikes hot, the silence deepens. The shrill of cicadas is missing.

Down we went through Fago where a camp of novices sat silent at their meal by the roadside. The pine woods became thicker, darker. The sun only just managed to send little spinners of light down through the trees into the pools of shade at their feet. The glades snowed butterflies; grasshoppers whirred from one grass stalk to another.

At the end of the steep descent through the woods we arrived at Camigliatello. Moccone and Camigliatello have grown, almost overnight, from a mere cluster of cottages into a trim little *villegiatura*. They are forest villages. The houses are all wooden, painted green, sky blue, grey and chocolate, and they all have sparkling tin roofs.

The two men who had brought us were a strange pair. One, who was tall and lean, bore a striking resemblance to Groucho Marx, with the same loping walk, and his wiry black hair looked like an unruly tea-cosy. When he took off his dark glasses one almost stepped back in amazement at the sight of his enormous staring eyes. His companion was a cherubic fellow in his late twenties whose florid face was in keeping with his calling, for his father owned the largest pork butcher's shop in Rossano. They were both frequent visitors to Camigliatello and no sooner had we stopped outside the café where the few week-enders congregate than they were surrounded by their friends and they invited us to join them for a drink. The bar, run by a bull-necked barman and a volcanic young lady who stared archly at the customers, boasted of a dance hall which offered amusement on very unfair terms: ladies were admitted for two hundred lire; gentlemen had to pay a thousand.

The drinking over, we announced that we were going off into the woods to pitch the tent. The two from Rossano would not hear of it. 'We've brought a wonderful picnic. Who is going to eat it all if you don't help us?'

Within half an hour we were sitting in the shade of pines near a fast-running stream. The feast was spread out before us. They had, indeed, brought enough food for ten people. There were spicy sausages that made us liberal with the chianti, a gigantic ham, squelching cheeses, crumbly cheeses, anchovies, olives, a golden pie filled with egg and hashed meat and, to finish, two huge melons.

Luigi, the butcher's son, cut his hand trying to open tins and juggled with them so much that the travelling rug he had brought was spattered with a soggy trail of tomato juice and gherkin water. Severo, under the influence of wine, began to mumble incoherently towards the end of the meal, then distinguished himself by leaning backwards where there was nothing to lean on and bowling down the slope. A boulder just saved him from the stream.

Both the men spoke so fast in their Calabrian dialect that it was difficult to follow all the time. A fuddled head jibs at dialects, and Calabrese is so breathy, explosive and clotted—you feel you are listening to Arabs talking Italian. Severo told a long story about an impossible love affair with a secretary from Rome whom he had met on the Tyrrhenian coast.

'She came to see me several times, but I had to go and meet her three stations away from Rossano in the car—I borrow it from the garage where I work—so that people wouldn't see us and talk. I couldn't tell my mother because she has picked out a girl for me already. It's as good as settled!'

Luigi was like a good-natured bear, shy and slow-moving. He was living literally off the fat of the land and even apologised for having brought so much food for the picnic. His tougher companion made him blush as he described his great rambling house in Rossano and the well-stocked shop. 'His father keeps a big dog. He's terrified of it, but it makes him look important!'

Though Luigi was not a victim of unrequited love, his conscience was weighted with other problems. His father, who was apparently able to pull strings, had arranged for him to avoid military service. This had made the boy the laughing stock of the other young men in the town. He didn't know what to think when I suggested the world might be a far happier place if no one did military service.

The two friends were in no hurry to get home to Rossano. In fact, they didn't know where to go or what to do, but sat waiting for something to happen, certain that the sky would make its decision and let them know. Though they had no plans of their own they did not lack suggestions as to how we should spend our time. Their ideas included an evening at the dance hall, with a big dinner beforehand—or a trip to Rossano, followed by night-bathing near Schiavonia. Neither of these proposals could woo us away from our determination to spend a quiet evening in the forest and, after a long verbal tussle, they saw they were beaten and sent us off with their blessing.

The cloying sociability of Calabrians, bred of being herded together, conceals, I think, a good deal of loneliness. The Southerner does not cultivate the hobbies and zests which round off the sharp edges of life and, to escape loneliness, he rubs shoulders with his neighbours, *ad nauseam*. Permanent unemployment or the odd job here and there—that is his lot. Those who are more intellectual fret in the humdrum of some minor official post and inevitably fall into a state of vegetative boredom, relieved only by prattle, card-playing and a portable radio.

The Southerner is constantly pitched right into the mesh of society. Where he lives in the street and in cafés, we live each in our secluded compartment and are nettled when the neighbour comes snuffling round our door. Life in a South Italian town is, in the fullest sense, public. The people do not live in glass houses, but they might just as well. A humiliation, a flare-up, a passion, a beating, a joke, are public property as soon as they are born and go zigzagging down the street to delight the ears of all. The place looks dead and buried—yet, because we see its menfolk eternally pacing the Corso or hanging round coffee bars, we must not think that this is their heart's desire.

One has only to talk to a Calabrian or a Sicilian for ten minutes to see that, behind all the froth and fume, there is real mental alertness. Quick-witted, wordy, they have understood you before you even open your mouth. It is exhilarating to see how they seize upon a point, elaborate it, juggle with it, and, with a final twist, serve it up to you again polished and enlarged to four times its original size.

South Italians are acutely conscious of things physical. They can tell at a glance if a girl's thighs are shapely, if a wine has body or if a plough will be deep in furrow, and they will describe what they see in ripe, joyful terms. We, who are muffled indoors for three-quarters of the year, are sly, apologetic sensualists.

Southern Italy has not yet fallen victim to mass-mindedness though this is making inroads on native judgment and originality. There is still vitality there, unquenchable, and truly personal reactions to life. That is why one rarely meets the dead-pan face and the dust-coated mind. But today this vitality finds no outlet in constructive living—and so the people have become soured.

Evening. The forest was still. A group of boy scouts were building a fire under the supervision of a priest. We passed them and were alone. Everywhere there were scents—sweet-water scent of wild strawberries, sun-warmed resin, birch syrup oozing drop by drop, shepherd's thyme crushed underfoot.

The light thickened and a bee zoomed by. The night wind had risen. It stirred the pines for a moment, then swooped and nodded the grasses.

Among the hart's tongue and bracken we found a place to sleep and lay looking up the long pine trunks where tree creepers spiralled.

CHAPTER FIFTEEN

The Forest

WE camped for two days in the forest. All day it was as cool and sweet as the heart of an apple. The sun, even at midday, never robbed the shade but flecked the leaf-mould with a shifting mosaic of light and shadow.

A stream bustled down not far from the tent, tunnelling under drifts of sphagnum moss. In some places it was honey coloured, in others so clear that you could hardly decide whether you were looking into air or water. I traced it up into a narrow gill where it gushed into a basin below rocks bloomed with black and powdery green lichen. There were plenty of birds to entertain us: spotted woodpeckers, stiff with tails squared against a trunk; long-tailed tits, all fluff and squeak; a paunchy bullfinch that came near to stare; and two flycatchers which kept watch in a glade.

The scouts paid us a courtesy visit one morning at the prompting of the priest, but they were so monosyllabic, unsmiling and full of adolescent shyness that at first communication was difficult. They were unable to get their huge billy-cans clean. We showed them that wonders could be done with wood-ash and this little camper's trick created a fellow-feeling. The boys became more talkative, though we never quite got past their barrier of aloofness.

I often had the impression when talking to Calabrians that I was near a coiled spring of energy that might be released by one touch or change of circumstance. These boys were silent, brooding. There was no horse-play; their high spirits were closely corked. The trouble was that they were intimidated by the presence of a woman. The super-virile Mediterranean man seems to find it very difficult to talk naturally to a woman, especially to a woman who thinks for herself. The men we met while travelling invariably addressed themselves to me as if I alone was capable of replying, and if they wished to ask L a question they always did it through me.

The day before we left Camigliatello we saw, sitting outside the central café, a man whose face seemed familiar. He was a salesman with whom we had had a chat on the roadside near Trebisacce, a grave, burly man whose thoughts were always leagues away from the matter in hand. His tendency to day-dream had got him into many scrapes with the company for which he worked but, on such occasions, the cloud which perpetually surrounded him was liable to lift all of a sudden and he would then be prepared to stalk into the manager's office, thump his square fist on the desk and refute the charges brought against him.

Here he was, tricked out in immaculate attire and sipping a martini. He was on holiday or, at least, his wife was, and he had called to see her. She was not visible; he had left her at the *pensione* to do some washing while he came out to take the air. We said we should like to see her and when he had finished his drink the three of us set out for Moccone, a mile away.

They were staying with some villagers in a house beside the railway station. Just in front of the door was a most unusual edifice—a corporation W.C. in which the cisterns chirruped and sang invitingly. The wife, a raven-haired, lissome girl with obsidian eyes, came from the kitchen to greet us and was followed by the old woman who owned the house and a group of young women and children who stared, shuffling and whispering among themselves. I was introduced as 'the man who keeps laughing' because my laughter was apparently what had impressed the earnest salesman most.

He had only been married eight months, but was already

Back street, Reggio

Tyrrhenian beach, south of Reggio

finding the yoke irksome, for he never lost a chance of making some slighting remark about womankind. While expressing admiration for what he called our 'adventurous spirit', he could not help adding, 'How lucky your lady is, though, to be shown all these places. She must be thankful!'

His wife was waiting for him to settle down, hoping that he would not spend too much time away from home or go on the spree, yet knowing that her fate would not be different from that of any other Italian woman. Up to the time of their marriage she had been a schoolmistress in the Vulture and, now that the first flame had awoken the woman in her, she was having to get used to the hard realities of domestic routine. Her attentiveness to her husband's every want betrayed anxiety. The knot in her breast would not be unbound until she had a child. Outwardly she was an ocean of calm; one felt it as she talked or sat listening, her hands folded. If true birth means passing from the security of a mother's love into a world where much is hurtful, then she had never been born. She kept with the tide, waited and watched.

When her husband asked if everybody in England got married in church we began to talk about religion.

'I was married in church to please the family and to please my wife,' he said, 'but wild horses would never drag me to mass.'

His wife didn't go to church regularly either, probably to please her husband, but she had something wise to say which, coming from a Lucanian woman, surprised me:

'If we don't go to church to marry there are terrible quarrels at home, and who wants to have the family as an enemy? We can always think what we like, you know.'

He was more outspoken against the church. 'They rule our lives, those priests, and because they are not sure of themselves they are always thinking up some miracle to impress us. There was an account of one in the paper the other day—an image of the Virgin that wept real tears. That's the way it goes—crying

Virgins, stigmata—and always in the South, you may be sure! How can people believe such rubbish?'

I suggested that the miracles were staged to divert people from thinking about their destitution. A silence followed and then the old landlady burst out: 'There will never be any miracles in England because you are all sinners!'

I was sorry to have offended the hostess but I was even more sorry to think that myths and miracles, well-founded though they may be, have to make up for the lack of a reasonable standard of living.

As we didn't want to burden the young couple with two more mouths to feed—whispering in the kitchen had told us there was some debate as to how to provide for us—we returned to the village to buy something for lunch with the intention of setting out towards Lake Cecita afterwards. The village store where all our shopping was done was kept by a craggy individual with a thick mop of hair. He was a grand salesman. Not content with a torrent of patter, he speared huge hams and whirled them round his head, juggled with glossy, swelling cheeses appropriately called *mammelloni*, rattled biscuits in tins, and with a flick of his finger sent olives flying out of jars for our inspection. His shop was a musical wonderland where everything jigged and wobbled, popped and tinkled. For our benefit he further enlivened his salesmanship with outbursts of swearing in English, the result of several years spent in a prison camp in Kenya. A more complete four-letter vocabulary than his I have never heard.

It was late evening when we neared Lake Cecita. The road wound through fields, lemon and rose in the fading light, and low hills which gave glimpses of creeks and inlets fed by freshets from the dense forests rising eastwards. Some of the hills bear trees—twisted pines and splayed apple trees rimed with moss. The hollows are full of them.

Just below La Fossiata, the thickest part of the forest, there is a dam that was built before the war to provide power for mines along the Ionian coast. The industry was never developed and now the dam throbs in the stillness, sending current through great overhead cables to Sicily. We stopped near the power-house. The sun sank over the lake—dead water deepening into violet. A lone fisherman packed up to go.

The trees grew too thickly for camping, and it was too late to venture up the steep forest paths in search of meadows. We went back along the road and then cut across fields southwards. Night shut down when we had only been walking half an hour and we had to set up the tent near the first coppice we came to. It was a cool, rustling night, the moonlight clear and cold. An owl swooped into a tree above the tent and sat listening for the scurry of mice in the dry grass.

CHAPTER SIXTEEN

To San Giovanni

THE wheezing *trenino* woke us. It shuffled past, bathed in steam, and rushed squealing into a tunnel. Some nuns appeared from nowhere and sat gossiping behind the pines and peering at us as we packed up the tent.

It was a fair walk to the road that leads to Bivio Garga and San Giovanni but the air was fresh and our steps light. We passed oak woods, already loud with bees, and came out into open rolling country where there were patches of potatoes and abandoned wooden cabins.

A jovial physical training master from Taranto stopped to give us a lift. His car was already full of peasant girls but they got out later at some deserted cross-roads and melted into the hills. 'They were too terrified to say a word,' he laughed. 'They just sat there blushing, not daring to breathe all the way from Longobucco. Our girls always think you are going to eat them!'

He looked far from terrifying and was himself a leader at a summer camp for children. The camp, to which he was going with the weekly supplies, was not on the road to San Giovanni and so he had to leave us to fend for ourselves again. The car disappeared up a stony track and we walked on to reach the shade of a solitary oak.

The sun was high. '*Arre, arre!*' A jet-black horse turned, clinking its harness, on the brow of the hill above the road. '*Arre!*' It strained and hunched forward as the share bit into the earth. A harrier flitted over, snake head twisting right and left.

Several cars went by—Milano, Roma—and put on speed when they saw us. The chink of a spade and a laugh made us look round.

'They are afraid of bandits!' A moustachioed roadman with an apricot face was smiling at us. 'They still think we are all bandits here! *Il cinema, il cinema ha fatto molto male!*'

I liked his boyish grin and tombstone teeth. He settled himself down beside us under the oak and rolled a cigarette, chuckling to himself. The harness clinked again on the hill. The horse turned.

'Look at the ploughman,' he said, 'under that sun!'

I said I thought the land was good in the Sila.

'Well, it is in parts but not here. It slips through your fingers. If only we had some of that rich Lombardy soil!'

'The road is good, anyway, in comparison with some we have seen,' I ventured.

'Oh, it's good enough. We haven't had it long and what a lot of trouble we had to get it! And this was made quickly compared to the others. Take the road to Villagio Mancuso, now. They almost finished it and then, as usual, something went wrong. The money didn't come through and we had to wait a whole year for the last four kilometre stretch to be completed.'

As he talked on I learned that he was from Cilento, the poorest part of Campania, and that he had come to work in the Sila when the land reform began. He was not very optimistic.

'Call it a reform if you like. They employ thousands up here on the "Opera Sila" and that's all right so long as the work goes on, but, once it is finished, what will happen? All those workers will be laid off and back where they started. There is another thing, too. They won't employ men who aren't of the right political colour. Some of my mates, whom you might call "red", got a job, but only because they came from far away and knew how to keep their mouths shut. If they had been locals no one would ever have taken them on.'

The peasants have naturally been eager to work for the Opera Sila, but there is not sufficient land available for all. So those who, for example, are engaged as day-labourers in construction will be high and dry when the Cassa per il Mezzogiorno winds up its activities—unless, of course, plans for greater transformations are afoot. Up till quite recently the landowners rented their land to the peasants who were always in debt. The landowners made only a moderate profit but they were content with this; it was easier to make a steady profit, however small, rather than improve the land. Improvement would have meant investing—and taking risks and good farming did not interest them.

The peasants paid for their 'privileges' mostly in kind. The farm hands on the large estates received a subsistence wage. I had heard something about the one-sided nature of the contracts and I asked the roadman if he could give me any details from personal experience.

'I am not sure what the conditions are in the Sila, but I can tell you what they are in my region. My brother works on a *masseria* and . . . well, guess what he gets—7500 lire a month plus a quintal of corn and forty kilos of beans a year! I don't know if you realise what that means. *Una vita di bestia!*' He spat and fell to twirling his spade which glinted in the sun.

Suddenly there was the sound of a horn and a shooting-brake came cruising along the road. The roadman sprang up, whispering, 'here come some of the big-wigs'. There were two men in the car and, as we were soon to learn, they owned vast tracts of forest in the Sila and were on an inspection tour. They agreed to take us to San Giovanni in Fiore, but made it quite clear that they were only doing so because they had seen us talking to the roadmender, whom they knew.

'I never take people as a rule, especially in this God-forsaken place,' said the driver who looked like a bad-tempered bull-dog. He showed himself to be, in fact, bawling and aggressive when he began to vaunt the merits of the 'good old days' under

Mussolini and to brag about the havoc his battalion had caused in Epirus. The other man, grey-haired and hook-nosed, was suave and sly, and tried to play the part of the distinguished man of the world to soften the bad impression given by his obstreperous lieutenant.

It was midday when we arrived in San Giovanni in Fiore. The name sounds well, but the 'capital' of the Sila does not come up to expectations. From a distance it looks like a flock of sheep that has come to rest on the brow of a hill. The decaying houses, round the outside of which run galleries reached by stone steps, are built of sheep-grey stone. Between them are narrow lanes where curtains of wool hang drying. Piles of rubbish litter these lanes, though behind the houses the rubbish has been swept into neater piles to make room for improvised bowling-alleys.

San Giovanni is a colourless town, sepulchral as the ascetic monk San Gioacchino wished it to be. He insisted that only *donne austere e irreprensibile* should live in the vicinity of the monastery, and today the old women in their black and white costumes look like crabbed old nuns.

In the eleventh century the Normans began to occupy the South, and Calabria, for the first time, was influenced by a Latin heritage and came under a feudal system. During this period San Gioacchino established his monastery in the Sila, guided, according to the legend, by oxen which St. John the Baptist revealed to him in a dream. Until his coming, the culture and learning of Calabria had been Byzantine. Cassiodorus, who won the protection of Theodoric, the Byzantine exarch, had copied and preserved Greek manuscripts. The monks of Rossano had gone out to carry learning to all parts of the empire and beyond its frontiers.

Today San Giovanni in Fiore is a town that has curled into its shell. Its windows stare, eyeless; its people stare and say nothing; its hens scratch; the wind flutters the rubbish in its streets. As you walk through these streets you suddenly come on to a wasteland of bare rock: the town has ended abruptly.

Beyond the wasteland lies a long ridge which shuts off any view of the Ionian. It is a dead end—nothing but hot, rocky walls—and to the west the view fades under a shifting haze of dust. The forests are far away.

Colour and joy must, however, break through somewhere and here, in San Giovanni, they materialise in carpets. The thirst for something bright sets hands fluttering and looms clacking inside the drab houses. In one courtyard I saw a carpet laid out in the sun, the colours deep and vibrant—plum, russet, black and violet. The same designs have been used for generations and, so I was told, they were brought to San Giovanni by Armenian settlers of whom the present-day weavers are descendants.

Lunch at the inn was ready by two o'clock. The innkeeper welcomed us, driving before him squawking hens that had hopped on to the landing to peck at sacks of grain. The half-open door of one of the bedrooms revealed a sagging iron bedstead across which a man was lying, snoring and twitching at each onslaught of the flies. The dining room was below in the cellar. It had been horribly modernised in sham red brick but the ceiling was untouched, a great pit of darkness from which one expected to see an owl peer down or a bat drop into the room.

The wood merchants, who intended to stay the night, had been assigned rooms in the warren above. When we arrived they were already sitting in the dining-room, fuming because lunch was late. There was nothing for it but to join them. They scowled at everybody, bellowed at the innkeeper, poked at their food with a show of disgust, and finally pushed their plates away when they were sure the other guests were looking. The meal was perfectly edible, but the innkeeper, with bated breath, suggested other dishes and tried to assuage his boorish guests by distributing extra paper napkins and uncorking bottles of his best wine.

The slices of melon which rounded off the meal cooled everybody down and we rose to go, the merchants to their rooms for a nap, and we into the town to look for a cobbler to repair our battered sandals. We found one in a hole-in-the-wall shop at the end of a dark slit of an alley. He had arched eyebrows and oyster-green eyes: it was like talking to a sea creature in its cave. He emptied his mouth of nails, slowly, and put in a piece of cheese that had been lying on the bench. His movements were calm and liquid and when he spoke his voice seemed to come from the black wall behind him.

The migratory urge had touched him, too, but, after spending two years in a shoe factory in some satanic town in Lorraine, he had come back, as they all do. 'I wasn't happy there—the people were not kind—but, then, I shouldn't complain because they let me earn my bread. One has no right to criticise another country if they give you work when there is none at home.'

CHAPTER SEVENTEEN

Ampollino

WE awoke to the swishing of an olive tree. A breeze had sprung up. The olive provides poor shade when once the wind has taken it: the sun scorched through the leaves and dinned in the brain. The fields of light, the silvery olives, the wind galloping over the rock—all reeled in a quivering dance of heat. The sun is a terrible master. One day it sucks all your strength away; the next it exhilarates, soaks into every pore until you feel you are being re-born, cell by cell.

San Giovanni was still visible on its ridge, though we had left it two full hours before and slept an hour at the roadside. The road played hide and seek with the town for several miles but still the town frowned down upon it. There was a stream below the olive grove and in its bed washing was drying—clots of rags, white, blue and red, that strained on the jagged rocks and undulated in the wind. Village girls, their work over, sat swinging their legs on the parapet of a bridge.

The cobbler had told us we might get a lift from a wood lorry and so it eventually turned out. A bone-shaker of a truck came along and, clinging for dear life to the chains which held the tail-board, we rode to Lake Ampollino. The lakes in the Sila are all deserted, even in summer, but Lake Ampollino is the loneliest of them all. Solemn and wild, it is a place to build a hut, to cultivate a plot and live a hermit. The lorry disappeared into the forest and the silence closed in behind it like water where a stone has dropped. The sloping lake shore was empty. Sheep droppings showed where flocks came to drink; there were the remains of a fire. Growing in boggy patches were horse-tails; tufts of lilac spurrey nestled between blackened pine roots exposed by the receding waters. Fish rolled white on a lip of sand and the lake, wimpled by the breeze, seemed to be flowing.

We heard the tinkle of cow-bells and saw a herd moving up from the lake towards the pastures on the steep slopes above. They were fine cows, dun and silver grey, with a curly nap between their horns and deep, quivering dewlaps. They threaded among the pines, halting to browse in the shade, and then, with a final heave, reached the meadow and sank into the spongy turf.

Men came along the shore, their faces as dark as their high black leggings. They began to talk to us but I was unable to understand what they said. I caught the opening phrase, but there our talk ended, and, after exchanging cigarettes, they went off, scrambling among the trees and hooting to hasten the cows.

In order to reach a road which would lead us anywhere we had to walk round the east end of the lake. The road wound below shaly cliffs shot with gleaming mica. We walked on, past another dam, and came to a low, red house which stood near the road. In the garden, which ran down to the lake, some men were sitting on a bench in the shade with a large decanter of wine on the table beside them. One was a haggard individual, all tics and squint—a state inspector of fisheries. Sitting next to him was a sort of walrus whose prickly face streamed with sweat. Both men wore suits which were limp with sweat and they seemed about to explode with the heat and the wine.

Conversation was slow and guarded. Mumbled consultations went on between the two men and a third, younger man who was lounging in a deck-chair and looking us up and down. A woman showed her face at the door and fled. Presently we were given lemonade and then, looking rather ill at ease, the younger man said: 'My wife is French. She would like to speak to you but she is shy.'

They began to call out in chorus: 'Maria! Come out and

speak to these people. Imagine a pretty woman like you being so shy!'

If her reluctance to appear had aroused our curiosity, this was soon dispelled when we saw her. She was a plump, sour-faced woman who had forgotten how to smile. Her French was half Italian and she spoke Italian with a very French accent.

'I was born in Algeria,' she told us, 'but I left with the whole family and came to Italy when I saw the country was going to become independent. You can't imagine what we suffered there.'

My refusal to be drawn into a discussion on the side of colonialism piqued her and, having no more to say, she resorted to the inevitable questions, asking how we liked Calabria. When I told her we had been very well received she snorted with contempt.

'They make me think of North Africans, these people. They are just born idlers!'

I was glad that none of those present appeared much inclined to keep us there. When we said we had to move on before dusk it was accepted without question.

'Born idlers'—her words stuck in my mind. I thought of the heat of the early afternoon. Is it surprising that all effort is snuffed out? The mind may teem helter-skelter with desires and plans but, in such a climate, one needs the strength of ten to climb a low hill, let alone scale peaks.

Had it not been for our hunger we would have camped by the lake, but the only shop nearby was in a village on the road to Cotronei and that meant turning east towards the coast. The village was a miserable collection of wooden huts set in a forest clearing. There was a school holiday camp there and we passed several troops of children, all dressed alike, parading rather than walking. Obviously footsore, they trudged forward in a wavering line, accompanied by older girls, also in uniform, who looked as bored and as tired as the children. Supper was waiting somewhere under the trees.

The shop was adjacent to a bar which had been suitably modernised to attract the staff of the holiday camp who would expect town amenities. The prices, too, had been arranged to coincide with the summer invasion; the owner, who tried to overcharge us, became very huffy when we insisted on paying the real prices.

Intending to spend the night near the village, we had just begun to look for a place to camp when a large black car drew up beside us. The driver asked if we were going towards Crotonei. I have never kept to a strict plan when travelling, because a plan rules out any chance of discovery, but when you rely on the Italian *mezzo di fortuna* even the ghost of a plan is out of the question and you are liable to find yourself in a region you had no intention of visiting. This can be rewarding—if you are a wanderer then you have no option but to wander— but at that moment we wanted to stay in the forest and this obliging individual was offering to take us away from it. We hesitated—a fatal thing to do in Italy where, if you don't make your intentions clear at once, you will certainly be cajoled into doing what the other person thinks is good for you—and in that moment of hesitation we found ourselves in the car.

The road twisted down in a long series of bends. The grass disappeared; the trees grew fewer and fewer; the air became thick and suffocating with the dry, ashy smell of thistles and scrub. Our hearts sank with the road. The forest had spoilt us. Just before we reached Cotronei we asked the man to stop. It was the last place where there were any trees. Below there was a sheer drop to the village which stood among stony fields.

We hadn't talked much on the way down. The driver whistled and smiled to himself or pointed out a few landmarks, but he seemed to have guessed that we were not of the ordinary run of tourists. When we got out of the car he said, 'It's not very beautiful here, but it's interesting if you want to see how people live. Believe me, they don't live well.' With that he drove off and all the evening I remembered his secret smile.

We were dog-tired and it was no joke stumbling through vineyards and scaling stone walls. At last we reached a grove of chestnut trees and cut bracken to make a bed. The earth beneath the bracken was like dust and had a smell of sulphur. The mosquitoes got into the tent long before we did and were waiting for us. Stars spun into view far out over the sea. There was laughter in the village below: someone was playing an accordion.

The sun sailed up, leisurely, from behind the curtain of haze that hid the sea. The valley of the Neto blazed white. Far, far away Santa Severina caught the first light—a chiselled stone with a castle on its back. The long waves of rock began to simmer; outlines blurred. Only the mountains to the south still held some folds of shadow. These mountains are called Femminamorta; against the morning sky they resembled a corpse under a shroud.

It was a short walk to the village which formed a little suburb of Cotronei. There was only one fountain and a long queue of people waiting to fill their barrels and buckets, so we had to make do with a quick wash. Even then an old man with a donkey cursed us, saying we were making his animal wait too long to drink. A big slatternly girl, wearing nothing but a black dress, monopolised the fountain for a good ten minutes despite the murmurs of discontent from those waiting behind. By way of conversation I asked her if any members of her family were abroad. Yes, she had a brother in Paris. 'Does he like living in France?' I enquired. 'He doesn't live in France, he lives in Paris,' was her reply.

Some old people had been watching us from a garden over the road and presently a man, barefoot and dressed in rags, came and gave us a handful of pears arranged on a figleaf. 'For the travellers,' he said, and turned away before we could begin talking to him.

Our washing over, a decision had to be made—to go down

to the coast or to climb back into the Sila. The car which had stopped the evening before had really taken us off our route. We wanted to see more of the Sila and, looking down into the liquid fire of the plain, we had not the heart to go on. Returning meant a gruelling up-hill climb, but forest and water mirrored in our minds and drew us on.

There was a dilapidated hut by the roadside, a shell of white boards topped by a rusty tin roof. A petrol drum leaned against the wall outside to catch any rain that didn't leak through the roof. Two beautiful amphoras stood on the window-sill and we stopped to look at them. Children were crying inside the hut and on the steps two little boys were playing with shining toy cars which looked like presents from America.

A woman bustled out and stood against the rickety balustrade, staring into the distance. She suddenly noticed us and gave a little cry of surprise. 'Foreigners?' she asked. 'Yes, foreigners.' 'And you are walking on such a day!' 'There is some shade on the road. It's not too hard.' 'Have you been through our village? What did you think of it?' 'It can't be much of a life here for you. Hardly anything grows.' 'Ah, no. I should think not. What hope is there for us? Look, just look where we live!'

Her arm encompassed the hut, the scrawny vines, the terraced fields set with grinning teeth of stone. 'And I have five children and a man . . .' her voice dropped, 'well, a man. He hasn't been back for three years.' She looked down at us silently, made as if to come down the steps to the road and then, perhaps because she felt she had said too much, changed her mind and turned to go into the hut.

'Good-bye. I must not keep you. It will be terribly hot soon.'

After walking three miles or so we had to stop and rest. Our legs seemed on the point of collapse, pushing up and up. I guessed it was nearly eleven o'clock.

A young doctor helped us on our way. He was driving to

a holiday camp to tend a child suspected of having scarlet fever. The car bounced up a track into the forest and stopped in the silent courtyard of a great stone house which had once been a monastery. There was a Greek Orthodox cross over the lintel. The doctor disappeared inside, his steps echoing on the stone flags, and we sat under the cool chestnut trees in the garden. A few children came to stare at us. They were not in uniform and told us they were free to do as they liked when games were not organised, though the afternoon siesta was compulsory.

An old gardener who was watering plants waited until the children had scampered away and then came up to speak to us. 'Where do you say you live?' He was a bit hard of hearing. 'In Paris!' His mouth dropped open. 'Why, I went there in 1926 to visit my brother. He was a waiter and a bit of a rip, too. He got me a ticket to go and see the "Folies Bergères." I'll never forget it. Ai, *che carne rosa!*' He shuffled off among his plants, chuckling to himself and sifting over his memories.

The doctor came out of the house. 'The child isn't very ill. It isn't scarlet fever, anyway.'

'What kind of cases do you mostly have to deal with round here?' I asked.

'Do you want to be here all day? Because it will take me all day to tell you! No? Well, there is no more malaria at least, thanks to Mr. Rockefeller, though many of the older people are weakened by it and unable to put in a full day's work. I get plenty of cases of typhoid, of rheumatic fever, especially in the autumn, and then there is ophthalmia among the children and, among the women, miscarriages and still births galore. I am up against village quacks who carry out abortions on women who have made a " slip ". Their faith in these old crones is unshakable and I get myself disliked for my interference.'

I mentioned the village with only one fountain.

'That's the trouble in Cotronei, too. The water supply is a disaster. What kind of hygiene can there be in such a place? Yet Cotronei is well served in comparison with some places.

Near Santa Severina there is a village where there is no water
at all. A tanker brings water for the village every two days.
Each person gets five litres, no more, and that has to meet all
their needs until the next delivery. Nothing has been done
about it since I came here, and that's four years ago.'

'You live among these people,' I said, 'and look after them.
Do you see anything new in their lives, any change for the
better?'

'I see despair. I hear complaints. I am father confessor to
most of them. It becomes an obsession. Every day I hear
the same thing—"What are we to do when the Ente Sila can
no longer provide work?" Improvements? Real improvements—none. You see, these people have never possessed
anything and when they earn regular money, as they do now
working for the Ente Sila, they spend it all at once on television
sets or motorcycles. In ten years they will be back in the same
state of poverty as before, mainly because the birth-rate here is
so high that any reform is a dead letter from the very start.
That's another question, the reform. Show me someone other
than a landowner who is satisfied with it. There are hundreds
of families here who got no land and who never will get any.'

'But I thought more land had been shared out here than in
any other region of Calabria.'

He bent his head, then, looking up with his serious dark eyes,
he said slowly: 'It is true, in a way, but they only gave the
fallow land. You saw the land I mean near Cotronei. Liquorice
grows there but precious little else, because it is full of stones.
They don't even bother to gather the liquorice now, and as to
trying to farm that land. . . . Of course, some peasants have
their own holdings at last but the authorities never attempted
to share equally. They made lists of names—the most "needy"
families were at the top of the list—and then the names were
written on pieces of paper and put into an urn. The peasants
concerned assembled and the first name was drawn, usually by
the mayor. The lucky man drew the next name and so on, but

many feel there was injustice from the outset and suspect that preference was given to some families while others were never enrolled on the original list. To me they all seem to be in need. Sometimes I succeed in curing their bodies, but I can't cure their basic illness—poverty.'

'What made you come to Cotronei in the first place?' I asked.

'I am from a poor region, too, from the Abruzzi. I studied medicine in Rome and worked in a hospital in Naples for some time, but I didn't like Naples. One day I heard a of vacancy here and took it. You know, the life of a professional man in South Italy is no bed of roses. The small towns are full of doctors who have no patients and lawyers who have no clients. There must be three hundred doctors in Catanzaro, and Catanzaro is no metropolis! I didn't want to become like them, frustrated, living on air and empty prestige, so I came here. There is plenty of work, both day and night. I don't earn much, but I learn and I am useful.

'My friends in Rome think I am crazy, of course. "Here comes the country bumpkin," they say. "Fancy burying yourself in Calabria above all places!" I wish they would come and see for themselves but, then, I doubt if they would understand.'

It was past midday and the doctor had to go on to the holiday camp that we had seen the previous day. The atmosphere at this second camp boded ill for the inmates. The director, a churlish old man, was on guard at the gate when we arrived. He leaned on a sturdy crab-stick which, when it was not being used to prop him up, must have struck terror into those under his care. When we asked a few questions about the camp he scowled at us, mumbled something about not understanding what we wanted to know, and stumped away, leaving us to the girls who were in charge of the children. They were brassy, hen-sure, and they bounced about and marked time as they talked to give some semblance of energy and zeal. They fell over themselves in addressing *il signor dottore*, but he was not impressed and confined himself to examining the daily sick-list which they had drawn up. It contained nothing more serious than colds and scratches.

The girls' chief complaint was that the children were lazy and would not walk, dirty but loath to wash. They had obviously come to the Sila expecting a holiday, only to find that they had been landed with a job which proved irksome. They appeared to take no interest in the children—being group leaders was simply an excuse to get away from home.

Over coffee I asked the doctor where the children in the camp came from.

'Mostly from villages on the coast, I think. Perhaps a few from Reggio. They all come from very poor families and they spend two weeks here free of charge.' 'And who selects them?' 'Generally the local priest.'

Educational establishments in Italy tend to be gloomy and regimented; recreation, too, often degenerates into drill. One sees too many shaven heads and uniforms, too many people who are ill-equipped for the task of looking after children. It is hard to criticise, though, if one thinks of British schools where bullying and mental anguish are a part of everyday school life.

The doctor had to return to Cotronei. He sped off up the road in his car, waving furiously. 'Come again,' he had said. 'Come again. My dog doesn't bark, so you needn't be afraid. He knows I am often desperate for a long talk!'

CHAPTER EIGHTEEN

Last Look at the Sila

LAKE AMPOLLINO was rippling. The road lay under pines, cool despite the sun. Near the shore there were two hide tents and a smoking fire on which an oil-drum balanced perilously. A grubby child with a bandaged head lay at the entrance to the tents; beside him dozed an old man, bearded and dressed in rags. A short way off a lorry was parked. The driver was sitting in the shade of a pine and staring out over the lake. His companions were repairing electric cables high up on the mountain.

'Are those people in the tent gipsies?' I asked him.

'No, they are not gipsies, they are just vagabonds. *Poverini*! *Non mangiano mai*. The old man and the child are ill. The others are scrambling up the mountain there to gather black-berries. Some fellow with a van comes up from the coast every day to fetch the fruit. He pays them fifteen lire a kilo. Did you ever hear of such exploitation! That's how they live all the year round, off blackberries, chestnuts, and doing any sort of odd job.'

He was from Cutro, and made me laugh when he told me that the people in Cosenza were *più gentile* than those in Catanzaro, his own province: a rare lack of local pride.

'It's a fine place, the Sila,' he said, settling back against the pine trunk, 'but you ought to see it in winter! We got completely lost on Botte Donato one February. Some main cables had to be repaired. There was over three metres of snow and a blizzard blew up just as we were getting ready to climb on to the pylon. We sat tight under the lee of a rock and waited for hours until the wind dropped. They had to send climbers up to get us. I was laid up for two weeks after that little expedition!'

The hills on the north side of the lake are almost bare. I asked the man if there had ever been any trees there.

'Yes, it was covered with them twenty years ago—great thick pines like you see in Fossiata. The Germans came and cut some down, and the English and Americans finished the work. They took away every bit of timber they could get to make bridges and whatnot and now you see the result—as bald as a bishop!'

There was no village marked on my map for many miles and our legs were beginning to feel like cotton-wool through lack of food.

'Is there any chance of getting anything to eat near here?'

'There is a shop, I think, at the cross roads near Bocca di Piazza, but that's a good two hours from here on foot. We'll be going that way later and if we see you we'll give you a lift.'

As it happened, we didn't need to take advantage of his offer, for a car picked us up a few miles farther along the lake. A young priest was driving, accompanied by a tanned, grey-haired man. This man seemed to resent our presence at first and sat silent, studying our faces in the mirror, his mouth fixed in a grim line. But eventually a thaw set in. The priest made a few shy attempts at humour which were spoilt by his nervousness. He stumbled over his words, blushed when spoken to, fidgeted in pockets for maps, repeatedly asked his companion the time and kept staring out of the side window at the wheels as if he expected them to fly off at any moment and run along beside the car.

There was a new 'Opera Sila' village on our route—Novale or Craso, perhaps—a group of neat houses painted pink and green. I could not help wondering how the inhabitants obtained supplies to meet their daily needs: there was no shop in the village and the nearest place at which anything could be bought was at least fifteen miles away. We stopped to look at the place and a village idiot, his face twitching, came up and asked for cigarettes. The priest blushed to the roots of his hair and fumbled in his purse. A five-lire piece was pressed into the outstretched hand and the man bounded away over the fields, gabbling abuse.

The silent man at the priest's side turned to us and said, in a rich Cook County accent:

'They really do some cadging round here, don't they!' He was a Chicago Calabrian who had left the Sila when he was fifteen. Having 'done' most of the countries in Western Europe he was now visiting the scenes of his childhood. The priest, who was a distant relative, had been commandeered to guide him, and was tired out—for the American was the kind of person who is capable of going for a five-mile walk and clipping the garden hedge before breakfast.

'Yeah, we certainly have got around. Padre here has really put himself out. I guess we must have done three hundred miles since yesterday morning!'

'Padre' clenched the wheel and smiled wanly. I tried to bring him into the conversation as much as I could, because once the American knew we spoke English he insisted on speaking it all the time. This troubled the priest, who knew no language other than Italian.

The American was the manager of a six-hundred-room hotel in Chicago, or so he maintained. Bland and rather patronising, well steeped in homely Anglo-Saxon virtues, he regarded business not merely as a means of making money but as a way of life. Though he liked to come back to Italy, he found a short holiday there enough and felt happy at the thought of being able to go home to a country where his acquisitiveness and drive were better appreciated.

'The people here are great but, God, how do they get on without doing any work?'

The way people in his native village lived did not seem to hold much interest for him. He did, at any rate, enjoy the landscape, though his comments never went beyond: 'Why, it's as pretty as a picture!'

Lake Arvo is different from the other lakes of the Sila. It is more truly Alpine, not so treeless as Cecita nor so gloomy as Ampollino. The mountains surrounding it are very high but they sweep back, making the lake seem wide. It is this impression of width that gives its banks a misty quality. They swell in loops of firm sand, darken where the pines come down, thrust out a stony foot where fish can lie in shade. Above the shore are meadows, trees, meadows again on the sky-line, a glossy crown of grass, all wind and light.

Lorica, the only village on the lake, is a holiday centre, yet it was practically empty when we arrived. Priest and pilgrim decided to go to the impressive state *albergo* for lunch. We followed their example and found the prices very reasonable and the food excellent. Everything was served on local ware; peasants danced round the moulded water jug and jigged on the edges of the plates. The room was cool, the floor scrubbed to chalky whiteness, and the walls were as blue as the sky.

Our two companions devoured half a chicken apiece and polished off two bottles of wine. They sat back exhausted. The priest's eyes were swimming behind his steel spectacles. The chicken had left a juicy dribble down his cassock which dried as we sat drinking coffee on the terrace below.

L kept the American at bay while I chatted to the priest. I have never found it easy to keep up conversation with priests. I always feel I am talking to someone who is on the other side of a glass door, and verbal paralysis results. The priests I have known were either so hail-fellow-well-met that they never allowed you to slip a word in edgeways or so mouse-like that you felt you ought to address them in a whisper.

Don Anselmo was of the mouse variety but, though timid, he was a kind and sincere man—one of those Italian priests whose understanding and real efforts to help the needy of their parish soften to some extent the harsh rigidity of Vatican doctrine.

Were it not for simple priests like him, anticlericalism might be far more virulent than it is.

He lived in a small village not far from Stilo. His church, he told me, was badly in need of repair and, as there was no house for the priest, he had to live with a farmer. 'We hope to build a house one day but I don't think it will be in my lifetime.'

I was curious to know if he had a large congregation. He laughed and reddened a little: '*Ah, molte donne! Sempre le donne!*' I concluded that the male population had no respect for the cloth and imagined him under its fierce scrutiny.

His dream was to go abroad, to Spain or France. '*Ma, è caro, troppo caro.*' I was under the impression that the car was his, for so many priests in Italy have cars, but he corrected me. 'Oh, no. My friend here hired the car specially for his trip.'

Though he could not boast of a car, he had rich relatives who owned a *palazzo* in Rome. He told me they had paid for him to take orders—he was an orphan—and paid dear, too, for rents are high when it comes to entering God's mansion.

Don Anselmo's voice was gradually drowned by outbursts of verbal vastness from his American kinsman. Above the trickle of words I had already heard a momentous description of the Grand Canyon and an awe-inspiring account of skyscraper car parks, but now the subject was Al Capone.

'If you are a Calabrian, people automatically put you in the gangster category. And they have all the wrong ideas about gangsters. I knew Al Capone well and a finer man you couldn't wish to meet. Do you know that during the depression he ran a restaurant where he used to feed over two thousand destitute every day at his own expense? He was a gangster all right, but he thought of others. A great guy!'

The hottest part of the day was over when we got on to the road again. From ten in the morning it is very hot but around three a cool wind springs up. The forests are thick under Botte Donato. As the road winds on, sometimes darting away from the lake, then coming up to it again until you begin to think there are several lakes, the carpet of pines grows sparser.

The sky is the great marvel of the Sila. Even in cloudless summer it changes often—morning mother of pearl, midday copper. When the wind rises the sky burns in icy greens and white sea reflections, settling finally into cornflower blue before darkening into night.

The priest wanted to show his friend Silvana Mansio—a calm backwater for visitors—and, turning off the main road, we reached a group of wooden houses set among lawns and orchards. They looked so much like 'isbas' painted red, silver and green that we seemed to have entered a set specially constructed for a fairy pantomime.

'It looks like something out of New England,' said the American, referring to the wooden church into which the priest had gone.

It was not far from Silvana Mansio to Camigliatello: there was the silver web of the lake again, peaceful in the evening light. In the village the priest stopped and shyly wished us well. The American unrolled himself from his seat and thrust out a hand like a two-pound ham:

'Glad to have known you. If you're ever over in the States. . . .'

The next day familiar faces greeted us in Camigliatello. We ran into the surveyor, still grinning and shaking his head at our foolish exploits. His wife had caught up with him—a woman built on generous lines and with a very determined look. Here was the reason for his permanent state of nerves. '*Si, carina. Credo di no, carina.*' She listened, unmoved, benevolent but condescending, until his sputtering came to an end. This was the moment to squash him and she never failed to do so.

'Rodolfo, my dear fellow, you know you are talking utter nonsense. When will you learn not to agree with me all the time?'

She was not in the least surprised at the way we travelled

about and, smiling roguishly, she exclaimed: 'It would have done him good to travel more when he was young.'

At the restaurant everybody was watching a tennis match on television and when we left most of the customers still sat in front of plates full of stone-cold spaghetti and congealed tomato sauce. We went out on to the road and looked back on Lake Cecita for the last time through the golden haze of the afternoon.

The Sila is beautiful enough in itself, but its beauty is trebled because it comes as such a surprise. It is one of those rare places where, within only a few miles, desolation miraculously gives way to cool plenty. It is restful, not too grandiose. There are no mountain crags to bar its horizon and it contains no deep, sunless valleys. Once you have climbed above three thousand feet you are in a great bowl of light, cut off from the world and neighbour to the sky, where the wind from the two seas stirs early and whispers so insistently that you are ready to wander till you drop if you love space and freedom.

CHAPTER NINETEEN

To Tiriolo

WE left the Sila on the back of a fish-van driven by two murderous-looking characters in striped blue and white jerseys. They both kept bellowing inaudible things at us out of the cabin as the van careered down from Monte Scuro pass. The van looked empty but during the downhill rush a box of sardines slithered out from under a tarpaulin and began to perform a jig. One good jolt was enough to turn it upside down. The fish slapped against our legs and cuddled up to the rucksacks until, by the time I managed to stow them away under the tarpaulin again, our things were in a fine mess. It was only when we arrived at Cosenza that I realised what the fish-mongers had been shouting: 'Sit *on* that tarpaulin!'

Cosenza smelt stale in the heat. The houses were shuttered as if the plague had seeped up from the river-bed. Garden palms hung limp. A film of dust roamed lazily through the streets. Lined up outside the empty market were handcarts. A pair of boots, worn right through to disclose a black circle of foot, protruded over the side of one of them. In it lay a man, hunched on a pile of sacks, his head lolling on to the rim of the wheel. The flies only left his mouth when he snored extra loud.

The villainous fish-mongers proved to be very friendly and insisted on treating us to a beer in a grimy little tavern near the market. There were only four or five men at the bar, but they were yelling at each other as if they were at a mass meeting. It is a way of forgetting the heat, an outlet for nervous tension.

A fat man who was sitting on a bench mopped his brow continuously. *'Fa caldo,'* he said (in a Calabrian's mouth it becomes 'far khaldor'). He chewed cigarettes instead of smoking them and the well of tobacco juice in his throat turned his voice into a croak. The barman mechanically wiped the wine slops from the zinc with a gummy sponge and stared into nothingness. The fat man began to pick his nose, gazing at the electrically-lighted madonna over the doorway. She floated on pearl-grey and violet taffeta in a fly-blown glass case.

There was a lull in the free-for-all. I heard muffled titters across the road. The shutters of one house were slightly open and in the slatted half-light I could see plump arms, breasts bobbing under foaming lace, the white flash of teeth. The fish-mongers saw me looking, grinned up at the windows and then winked at me. *'Attenzione! Non è per Lei!'*

The shops opened at five o'clock. A good half-hour before they opened there was a group of people waiting outside Standa, ready to rush in and enjoy that air-conditioned haven. We went into a photographer's to buy a new film. The manager, a thick-set man whose moustache was brushed into tufts over his cheeks, was pained at the sight of our sweaty faces and sagging knees.

'Put down your rucksacks; here behind the counter. What a weight! Ah, you young people!'

He was not much over forty himself, but his concern for our welfare was quite paternal. After giving the indispensable details of our journey we somehow got round to talking about languages and he suddenly brought out a phrase in perfect Russian, to which I replied in the imperfect variety. He was as delighted to find someone who knew a little Russian as I was surprised to find so good a Russian speaker in a small Calabrian town. There was no mystery attached to his knowledge. He had spent three and a half years in the Ukraine and White Russia during the war, whether against his will or not I was unable to discover. Even if his sympathies had been with the German army he had since found it politic to become a Communist. His linguistic attainments were due, he remarked wryly, to the patience and devotion of one of his mistresses, a Russian village school-teacher. 'It's amazing what one will learn to win a woman,' he said.

While we were listening to his account of love in the steppes, a man came in to collect the films he had had developed after returning from a trip to Moscow. Train-loads of Italian Communists leave for Moscow every summer. The round trip, which lasts two weeks, costs about £90. Needless to say, only well-to-do people can afford it and one wonders whether the 'lure of the East' is for them a question of deep conviction or simply curiosity.

People were just leaving work when we got out on to the road again. There was a steep two-mile hill to toil up and we were soon soaked in sweat. The road was narrow and the buses and lorries that roared by in skin-searing proximity left clouds of exhaust behind them. At last a young lorry driver stopped on the crown of the hill and shouted down: 'Where are you going?' 'Towards Rogliano.' 'Come on up.'

The cabin was stacked with round, flat loaves sprinkled with flour. At every jolt they cascaded down and set us all sneezing. The boy, who looked no more than sixteen, was relieved that we spoke Italian. 'You see, the other day I took some Scandinavians all the way to Pizzo and they didn't say a word to me. I like company when I am driving.' With loaves joggling on our heads, our knees jammed in among the controls and the engine boiling under our feet, we didn't provide very brilliant company.

Rogliano was nearer than I had expected. The road ran through a valley where orchards offered admirable camping sites, but after the ridge on which Rogliano stands, it began to climb rapidly and then suddenly pitched into a deep, wild valley, the valley of the Savuto. The dusk closed in. Far below the river rushed over iron-grey shingle, baleful and cold in shadow:

the cistus thickets were eerie and silent in the blanched light.

On the crest which overlooked the valley on the other side I saw a few fields and asked the driver to stop, for here was our only chance of making a camp before the light drained away altogether. At the side of the road there was a fountain and near it a marble sanctuary like a sentry-box which leaned perilously over the edge. The plinth had been shattered by a passing car and the madonna in the niche had turned her face to the wall, disowning road-hogs and pedestrians alike.

The search for a place to put the tent proved fruitless: there was nothing but stubble, brambles and stones. An angry swish among the tangled grass told me that a snake had settled before us in the only practicable place, and so we decided to sleep under a fig-tree.

The fields we had entered were at the foot of a rampart and behind the rampart was a little town, Carpanzano. Windows began to light up in the rock wall until it glowed like a fairy hill. It was not easy to sleep that night. A wind blew up and growled in the fig-tree: its leathery leaves clacked. Our sleeping bags were wet through next morning. At dawn the valley was milky white with mist but, within an hour, it cleared away and the quails set up their cry on all the hills.

Two women, a mother and her daughter, stopped at the fountain to refresh themselves while we were washing. They set down the panniers in which they were carrying tomatoes to market and guzzled under the jet, scooping water into their bosoms. The mother had a wall-eye and wild strands of white hair covered her face. She spoke in whispers—not out of shyness, for she held herself proudly, her head thrown back. The girl, a baby-faced creature whose dirty, frayed dress was almost splitting over her plump thighs, was also quiet-spoken. She tried to explain in more understandable Italian what her mother was saying in Calabrian dialect. I had never heard anyone do this before—the general attitude being, if you don't understand Calabrian, too bad, you will learn.

Though in no way sophisticated, the girl had been living in Genoa for two years and worked in a shop. Life in a cosmopolitan city had had some effect on her, because she was conscious of her appearance. 'I don't dress like this in Genoa. I wear shoes there!' she said, laughing. I asked her how she liked the people in the North and she replied, with a peasant's good sense, 'Oh, I can't complain. There are good people there as well as here.'

The mother stood looking at us sadly. When her daughter came home she had the delight of seeing her as a country girl again and could pretend that she had not changed; but now we had appeared, the girl was talking about her new life and the mother felt estranged and uneasy.

'I had a son,' she said, 'who was killed in the war.' The girl looked hard at the ground. 'There is another son . . . away. We don't hear often.'

She had had to make what is, for a Calabrian village mother, a supreme sacrifice: she had sent her daughter away to work. Today this is still a last resort. Women must stay at home and marry locally if possible. The girl who leaves is suspect; tongues wag. But, gradually, girls who have sufficient spirit are breaking the bonds—though, in Cosenza, I heard that the assistants in Standa are despised and classed as any man's meat.

The mountains which run the whole length of Calabria heave into the rocky muscle of the Sila and then come to a sudden halt at the narrowest part of the peninsula between the gulfs of Squillace and Sant'Eufemia. The last bastion of the Sila, through which we were travelling, is still high, over three thousand feet, and four rivers rise there. The road curves along its western edge through forests of chestnut and oak, scored by gulleys where the thickets form such a compact mass that an axe would be needed to cut through them. The forest is dry and bristling under the sun. If you venture into one of the ravines you feel that you will never get up the other side—and

you know that, even if you succeed, you will be faced with
another and another. There is a whole tangled sea of roots and
tearing thistles to cross, fortresses of kermes-oak, wall after wall
of stiff cistus.

Half the morning had gone by the time we reached a house
at a level crossing where the little diesel train scuttles through
on its way to Catanzaro. We had been walking for several hours
and were glad to rest a while. A train went up the line and
when the gate swung up again there was a car waiting to go
through. The driver bowed stiffly in reply to my *buon giorno*.
He hesitated, took a good look at us and then offered to give us
a lift. He was oiled and powdered, wore kid gloves for driving
and sported an ornate gold tie-pin and gold cuff-links. He sat
very straight, as if he had swallowed a broom-handle, and when
he inclined his head to catch what I was saying I expected his
neck to twang rustily.

The perfumed Turkish cigarettes which he chain-smoked, and
the way he swerved round every bend in the road, eventually
proved too much for L. We asked him to stop so that her
feeling of nausea would pass off. Instead, he produced a flask
of brandy and with a gallant flourish poured out a thimbleful,
congratulating himself on his wisdom in providing for all
emergencies. It took only a short time to cover the last few miles
to Tiriolo. The man left us on the outskirts of the town; before
he drove away he gave me his card, from which I saw he was a
lawyer, one of the Cosenza fraternity.

There is nothing to be seen of Tiriolo as you approach it from
the north. Suddenly the road dodges round a hill and runs
along a rocky spur. Tiriolo is built on this spur in a com-
manding position between the two deep gorges of the Amato
and the Corace. Along the parapet, shaded by plane trees,
which overlooks the ravine sat a lot of old men. Some leant
on sticks, gazing silently into the heat; others swapped gossip
or mouthed to themselves. All stared at us and replied to our
greeting with a long, ragged volley of *buon giorno*.

On the other side of the square two portly matrons in costume were selling tomatoes and grapes under a tattered awning. They drew themselves up proudly as we came near and, with gap-toothed grins, invited us to photograph them. Their costumes were red, white and black, their skirts wide, and beneath the rucks of their blouses their ample bosoms roved at will.

Outside a café a massive, jowled man was holding a group of old codgers in suspense. His voice boomed, vibrated, sank to a whisper, grew languid, then rose to a shrill whinney, and as he told his story—a story about the war—his audience never took their eyes off his face. When his voice grew hushed they drew in their breath; when he bellowed their eyes started from their heads; and when he waved his fat hand, raised his eyebrows and slipped in some cutting phrase, they hooted with laughter and slapped him on the back.

This man, with his mobile features, eyes as black as buttons and crimped hair, once ginger but now a mottled grey, was an unofficial town story-teller. For the men gathered about him, his stories were more vivid than anything that radio or cinema could bring—because they knew every stick and stone of the local places he mentioned, enjoyed his slighting allusions to local landowners, and were beside themselves with delight when one of the company was singled out for ridicule and his past wrongdoings brought to mind. A Rip Van Winkle at the story-teller's elbow acted as both foil and prompter and brought out a bawdy quip of his own from time to time to please the gallery.

I don't know if, in Calabria, there are still story-tellers like those in Arab countries who invent tales out of whole cloth or whose art is built on folk legend. This one-man show, at any rate, was impressive even though the material used was local and largely topical—which made the whole thing resemble a game still to be found in South Italy, the *passatella*. This is a kind of verbal tournament in which everybody can take part.

A story is built up on actual happenings, embroidered and exaggerated. The person who distinguishes himself by his eloquence is declared 'king' of the group, and thus gains the power to offer drinks on the house to all his friends while openly denying them to his enemies. The atmosphere becomes tense after so much hard drinking and bouts of card playing; quarrels flare up and knives are sometimes used to settle them.

On this occasion there was only unrestrained jollity and they were all so carried away that they hardly noticed our presence. There was no room to sit outside and so, tired of standing, we went into the back parlour of the café to treat ourselves to an ice. The room was empty except for two melancholy card-players who perhaps had heard all the stories many times before. Not a leaf stirred outside. The frenzy of the cicadas broke in waves against the closed windows. The greasy cards snapped on the table; the ice-cream machine purred.

At last a girl came to see what we wanted. She was a most striking creature, with blue-black hair rippling to her waist and eyes so dark-fringed that you seemed to be looking into two anemones. Her legs were firm, bronzed, and she walked high-stepping, conscious of her beauty. I asked if she knew of a restaurant where we would not be fleeced too outrageously.

'You won't find what you are looking for here. There is only one restaurant and all the big cars stop there. Go up to "Ai Due Mari"; you will get a good meal there and not too dear.' She offered to keep our rucksacks and stowed them away in a hole under the stairs, swearing solemnly that they would be safe.

The restaurant was on the ramparts, high up in the town. As we crawled up the hot road towards our lunch a strange procession passed us. First, a fat woman, carrying an enormous sideboard on her head, walked with swinging, effortless strides, as straight as a ramrod. After a few minutes—for we stopped to gape at the spectacle—a young woman followed with the sideboard drawers piled on her head, and in her wake tottered a small boy, bearing the marble top. He had less success as an equilibrist: swaying and groping along the rough stone parapet, he finished up by chipping some fine chunks off the slab. I picked up one chunk and put it into his hand, at which he gave me a fiendish grin and a big wink as if to say, 'Ah, these women! The things they get you to do!'

Just below the restaurant, but thankfully out of nose-range, was a cave in the rock occupied by three woolly pigs. At least, I thought they were woolly—until I realised that the wool was a jacket of flies. But peace and fragrance awaited us on the terrace of 'Ai Due Mari'. It was overhung with a vine from which cascaded knot-grass, heavy with bees. Cool eyes of passion flowers shone where the shade was thickest.

The host was a charming man, unhurried, simple. He was surprised to see visitors, but he set to work with a will and prepared so copious a meal that we could not eat it all. He plied us with iced water—a rarity in South Italy—and served a bottle of wine so crisp and heady that it would have put mirth into a Swiss banker with stomach-ache.

The view from the terrace was impressive despite the heat-haze. The green plain of Sant'Eufemia flows in from the west, and eastwards spreads a vast, dry valley coiling towards the sea. The rift is not wide: barely five miles away rise the bald tors of Borgia and Cortale and, beyond them, roofed with cloud, is Aspromonte.

The splendid meal was coming to an end when a handsome young man came up to our table and asked if he might keep us company. He was the host's brother who had returned from the north of France for the *festa del paese*, a gathering of the clans which no Italian expatriate likes to miss too often.

'I come back at this time every year for the town festivities. It is expected of me and, in any case, if I stayed in the north of France all the year I would go round the bend. *Che vita laggiù!* We never see the sun, only smoke, bricks and fog. Tiriolo is a paradise after that!'

He spoke very good French, though he had only been in the

country two years. He told us in a half-serious, half-mocking way about his routine life at the factory and his fruitless attempts to make contact with the local people.

'The only real friends I have are Poles. I live with a Polish family and they have tried to teach me some of their language, but I can't get my tongue round those words!'

'What do you do in your spare time?' I asked.

'There is nothing to do there, nothing at all. I go home on my motorcycle every night and stay in my room reading—I have to improve my French, you know. Sometimes on Sunday I go fishing and I have been over into Belgium several times to buy things which are cheaper there. I am lucky in having a good room for which I pay very little. Some of us, Italians I mean, live in bad conditions. There are flats available, but rents are high and we are paid less than French workers. I know several Sicilian familes who can never pay their rent and who are often without gas and electricity because they can't meet the bills.'

There was no real reason why he should have left Tiriolo. The restaurant would have been his one day and he could have managed it with his brother, but he did not like that kind of work.

'Besides, it would mean looking after the land we own in the plain, and stooping in the sun to pick tomatoes isn't my idea of amusement—the ground is too far down! Now one field is rented by a market gardener who gives us part of the produce; the others are all overgrown.'

The chief cause of his dissatisfaction with Calabrian life was social. He had loved a girl in Tiriolo, but her parents had opposed the marriage and forbidden the two to meet. Disgusted with the whole set-up he had packed off to France.

'But things have changed here since I went away. You see girls and boys arm in arm in the streets sometimes. Love is less secret. I think it is because more foreigners come here and the young people follow their example. With me it was a different story. I never so much as touched the girl, mind you. We just went out together occasionally. I always respected her. Then, all of a sudden, her father started to prevent her from meeting me. Perhaps I should have insisted but, in our society. . . .'

This apparent shyness has nothing to do with scruples. If a man treats a girl as if she were cut glass it is usually because the relationship has become so public that there is no going back. A sharp distinction is made between the girl one marries and those who are temporarily useful.

I suggested that his reluctance to touch the girl, as he put it, seemed a trifle old-fashioned.

'You may think so, but it is question of honour! I have a sister and if I knew any man had made free with her, I'd kill him!'

'I am twenty-nine,' he went on. 'I'll have to find a wife somewhere soon.' He spoke so seriously and looked so glum that I had to smile. I smiled even more when, bewailing the fact that so many things had gone wrong in his life, he said:

'But I have always been a queer fellow—different, somehow. Do you know, even now when I go home late in the dark I am always afraid someone is following me! I run up to my room and shut the door quick when I get home!' What he needed was a purposeful girl to follow him home regularly. I could not quite make out this husky, seemingly self-possessed character who was afraid of the dark and crossed in love.

It was cool wandering in the narrow streets of the old town. Outside a church I noticed a large bronze plaque put up in memory·of 'the martyrs of the Hungarian revolution, 1956'. Beside it was a fountain, run dry, and the nearest usable pump was two streets away. People hailed us on every side. Youngsters came running up to ask for stamps. A bent old woman—she must have been eighty—trotted along beside us, peering into our faces and inquiring where we were from. She had bright eyes like a robin and her joints were still supple.

I gathered that she wanted news of some relative who had disappeared abroad. Surely we knew Enzo? Anyone from abroad would know Enzo.

At that time in the afternoon Tiriolo seemed to be peopled entirely by women. In most small Calabrian towns one sees only women and grey-beards; the younger men have nearly all gone abroad. The women stay at home looking after troops of children, waiting, half believing that their man will come back. As visits become less frequent and often cease altogether, the wife seeks consolation elsewhere. And she finds it, if her beauty has not been quite destroyed by child-bearing, in a temporary, guilt-haunted liaison with one of the few young men left in the village. The local papers often bear the sad tale of dramas arising from such whirlwind passions. People gossip; the husband hears rumours. The young man tires of a woman, who, from being a pleasure, becomes a burden. When lying and concealment can no longer bear the strain, when grief has screamed itself hoarse, these people have recourse to the knife.

We passed a little old mouse of a woman who was making *torchon* lace. The lace was stretched on a cushion and, as the dangling bobbins clacked, she nodded her head and sang to herself a tiny, buzzing song.

The women had got wind of our arrival and in every house they jostled at the windows to see us go by. Girls left their sewing; mothers came to the door, dandling infants. At one point a group of women barred the way.

'You are not going to escape,' they said. 'Stop and take our photograph.' None of them was over forty, yet some looked like ghouls—white, hollow-cheeked, flat-chested, the more corpse-like because they were dressed in black. I photographed them while a flock of children looked on, expectant faces all tilted upwards like daisies in a field.

One of the older women, a corpulent matron with a ready wit, came forward, bursting with pride, to write down her address—because she was the only literate representative among them.

In another street a tall woman was washing a child in a battered iron bath outside her kitchen door. Beside her was a younger woman, pregnant, whom I took to be a neighbour. It turned out to be her daughter. Grandmothers of thirty are not rare in South Italy.

We found a short cut to the main road, but were waylaid at the last house by a cross-eyed gentleman who beckoned to us. His wife, dressed in a dingy housecoat, peeped out and immediately took refuge in the kitchen. After the flurry had subsided inside a girl sidled out, followed by a young man who walked like a felon to execution. They both looked very embarrassed. The girl hung her head and the boy grinned, not knowing what to say.

'This is my daughter and that is her fiancé,' explained the father. 'He wants to go and work in France. Do you think he has a chance of doing well there?'

I imagined the first flush of passion after the wedding day, then the long absences, the fretting wife, the husband in some awful mine. They looked so young, the girl so fresh. I thought of the frightening spectre I had just seen up the road.

Nothing had changed at the bottom of the hill when we went to retrieve our rucksacks. The same men were sitting along the wall and had been joined by others. The town talker was absent, though: he had gone home to rest his tongue in readiness for the evening bout of story-telling. A hundred pairs of eyes were fixed on us as we passed and we could hear some of the comments: 'And a woman, too, carrying a bag! Wouldn't you think she could be better employed at home!'

The sight of a woman, or even a man, carrying a rucksack along the road places country people in a dilemma—they don't know whether to be concerned or outraged. Concern usually wins the day, for they themselves would never walk a mile along a hot road. They would either wait until the cool hours or borrow somebody's donkey—which, after all, is very wise.

As a wanderer you are an object of curiosity simply because you wander—many people asked, 'but why have you come here, when you could stay at home?'—and because in Calabria wandering is associated with gipsies and the workless. That you are a foreigner is taken for granted—no Italian ever goes about like that—but the strange thing is that you haven't a car or that you didn't come in an excursion coach. That takes some digesting. It is digested, however, and you are always welcomed and accepted. People may be surprised, but they will trust and help you.

Part Three

CHAPTER TWENTY

Sant'Eufemia

THE plain of Sant'Eufemia laps the foot of the rocky eminence on which Tiriolo stands. The fields of maize and melons roll inland and through them pulses the deep green Amato, bound for the sea. This two-way flow is a wedge of Tyrrhenian luxuriance driven in between the mountains.

We came to the turgid river. Oxen trailed along its sandy shore; its sallows silvered in the wind. On the bridge a man offered to take us part of the way along the new highway which runs from coast to coast. His silky manner and shining Mercedes gave me to think that he was a local official; when he got out of his car he treated us to a pious little lecture on the theme 'help one another', which he capped with a short account of all the religious medallions hanging on his dashboard. He turned off to go to Maida, leaving us at the crossroads. Vineyards and orchards stretched on every side and over them all, to the north, a pile of white stones blazed on a hill—Nicastro.

The day's work was over. Long lines of blue and yellow carts were moving towards the town, driven by tanned farmers who nodded gloomily as they passed, while their wives and daughters turned to stare fixedly at us. They then faced about again to jog in cadence with the horse's rump and wagging ears. Most of the horses were just skin and bone. One, especially, would have found the knacker's stroke a happy release. Its withers were so galled that the blue skin showed beneath and its crupper was all striped with the lash.

The furrowed earth under the orchard trees gave little promise of a good night's rest, so we decided to walk back a few miles and look for a better spot. We were about to leave when we noticed a very old man on the bank beside us. He had come up silently, as if out of the ground, and he sat leaning on his stick, watching us. After inquiring gently about the purpose of our journey—just enough to whet his imagination—he fell to contemplating the road, which was empty now that the procession of carts had disappeared over the hill.

'Would you like some fruit?' he asked after a long silence. 'Go over to the orchard there and take what you like. All the trees are mine.' The trees were loaded with juicy nectarines. We filled our pockets and returned to the shady bank. The old man was in some doubt as to what to do next. He mumbled to himself and rummaged in the pockets of his overalls. He obviously thought we were in a terrible plight and yet could see no way of helping us.

Eventually he got up and invited us to have a look at his *barraca*. 'It's here behind the orchard. Come in and have a little drink. I don't often see strangers.'

The barraca, which stood among fig-trees and vines, was nothing more than a barn with heavy double doors. The old man led the way, looking as frail as the almond tree in his yard. There was a domed well, bright blue, from which he drew water for us to wash. While we splashed in the cracked bowl—which the hens eyed jealously, for we were certainly usurping their drinking trough—he disappeared into the house. When he came out he was carrying a jug of wine and two of the grimiest glasses I have ever seen. They were covered with a crust of dried wine blotches to which fly-blow and grains of dust adhered in a close-packed layer. Had you dropped them the dirt alone would have saved them from being shattered. The wine, anyway, was excellent. It coursed straight to the head, quickened the sight and sent tongues of flame along the veins. He drank, too, throwing his head back and closing his eyes, and then he watched us drink, proudly, like a doctor who has given his patient a draught that he knows will bring relief.

Conversation with him would have been superfluous. He was a person who did not need to enter the shallows of small talk; he lived deep within himself and his silence, being a part of him, was not oppressive. Though he had reached the stage where it is difficult to accustom oneself to the fleeting impressions of life, to newness of any kind, he still had dignity and vigour of spirit. He must have been an alert man once, but somewhere a nerve had been cut: his brain raced but his hands trembled and refused to obey.

When he did talk it was about his dog, a kind of animated rug that lay panting in the heat, smiling to itself in its sleep. The dog was his only companion: his wife was dead (this much I did learn) and his sons were living in Argentina. The years of loneliness showed in his eyes, and doubt and regret as well. We had revived memories which he thought were permanently laid.

The topics of the moment were exhausted—the dog, the drought, the new highway from Catanzaro. Unable to contain himself any longer he said:

'Where are you going to sleep to-night? There is my house, but . . . you can't sleep in my room, not the two of you, I mean.' The door stood open, letting in the only light—there was no window. Inside could be seen a low wooden bed covered with a straw pallet, a table, a bench, and, leaning against the wall, a worn-down broom which was used for sweeping the earth floor. I told him that he need not worry on our account and that our tent would be quite sufficient.

'There is always the hay-rick,' he said, still trying hard to help. But the hay-rick was more of a dunghill than anything else.

The old man, as if he felt defeated in his first surprise encounter with the outside world for many years, looked confused; to hide his confusion, he began to weigh up, one by one, the balls of wine-lees which stood in a row near the wall. 'They use them for medicine hereabouts,' he said, 'and we send them to the big cities, too.' Then, slowly, as if to himself, he added: 'It is a pity I can't do anything for you. It's not safe for you round here alone.' To cheer him up a little I suggested we drink another glass of his miraculous wine together before setting out.

He came up the road to see us off and the dog, feeling that the occasion called for a show of politeness, came too.

'*Buon viaggio!*' The lonely blue figure stood for a moment with the sun behind him and then shambled back among the trees.

The woods that I thought I had seen from the car proved to be a mirage. We walked back several miles and found sandy bays running up into the hills, but the paths leading from them came to a sudden stop in a vast tangle of brushwood. Near the road was a new building. A large sign outside bore the one word 'Dancing'. I cannot imagine who would go to such a place to rumba and romance, but the window-boxes and the highly polished dance-floor showed that the optimistic owner was expecting droves of revellers from somewhere.

It was tempting to try and get into the place, so as to foil the mosquitoes, but there was nobody about whom we could ask except a small boy who ran away when we spoke to him. At least there was a pump under a cool carob tree and water to refresh us. The carob is a blessing brought by the Arabs to Sicily whence it spread to parts of Calabria. Its broad leaves give welcome shade in a parched land and its massive trunk is always moist, even in the hottest spells. The long ribbon seed-pods were ripe on this particular tree and we munched the pulp which surrounds the seeds as an hors d'oeuvre before supper. It tastes a little of banana, but is dry and sweeter.

The freedom of the hills had been denied us, the comfort of the 'Dancing' also, and so we had to look round for other accommodation. On the other side of the road, where the valley flattened out and stretched away southwards, there were some high cane-brakes. The bamboos, fluttering shafts of light, bent in the wind and hummed their quiet, hollow song. Behind them was a hay stack and a threshing floor. We dumped our bags on the chaff and were just complimenting ourselves on having found such a soft bed when hoarse growls came from farther down the field where some peasants were sitting in a reed hut. As we showed no willingness to decamp, the growls became more menacing. Then I saw one man brandish a knife.

Now peasants are notoriously touchy about their land—understandably so in Calabria where they have precious little of it—and if they suspect you are going to damage their property they are likely to get rough. When I see people getting hot under the collar in such circumstances I find that it is better to go up to them and explain what I want, showing that I intend no harm.

The overseer, who was so livid that I expected him to rush at me, calmed down when he learned that we were foreigners and invited us to sit at his table. The men were eating water-melons, hence the knives, and the whole hut looked like a butcher's shop spread with hewn carcasses of fruit. The table was swimming with red juice from which sodden flies were trying desperately to escape, raising their legs in slow-motion and shaking their wings.

We were told that we could camp there for the night and while we were setting up the tent we saw the overseer drive off in a trap. Some men went with him; the others walked.

At dusk the wind died. The bamboos stood motionless. Mosquitoes rose in whining clouds from the marshland and successfully sabotaged any rest that the straw had promised.

Next morning the tent was wringing wet. The sun stewed the moisture from the soil until the whole plain seemed one great vapour bath. No matter how much you gasped, you were slowly stifled and left like a limp rag, parboiled.

The peasants came back with the sun and began ploughing, stumbling bare-foot over the wet sods behind an ox that moved with clock-work steps, giving a great toss with its head each time it turned. One man, whose clothes were in tatters, took a particular interest in us. L played her flute for him and he left the plough and offered to make a flute for her there and then. The canes lying nearby were examined thoroughly. He cut one, lamenting that it was male. 'You need a female to make a good pipe.'

Within a quarter of an hour his square, earth-grimed hands had whittled the reed into shape. He held it delicately, feeling for the places where the holes should be pierced, and, as there was no hot iron available, he cut them with his knife. The pipe, when finished, played tolerably well but he was dissatisfied with it. 'When I was young I could make splendid flutes but now I have lost the touch. Somehow, all the music has gone out of me.'

The farm on which these peasants were working is one of the largest in the plain of Sant'Eufemia. They came to the fields every day from San Antioco, eight miles away.

'The master lives in a great house near Nicastro,' said the flute maker. 'He has no children and, believe it or not, though he is rich, he is no better dressed than I am. I'll guarantee he is one of the richest men in Calabria, but he lives like a monk. All his money is in banks in the North or abroad. His house is neglected and he won't spend a lire to improve his land. Look how we have to work! Do you think he would buy a tractor? No fear! A plough and an ox and a damn good sweat is all we get.'

These men were all Communists and bitterly critical of the Church. 'The clergy!' scoffed one. 'What good is their charity to us? They have seen to it all these years that we remain ignorant. But now we are waking up. We know from what emigrants say, and from the television, that other people live better than we do, and work less.'

Calabrians may feel that they have always been rejected and despised—but they have not, as yet, taken to despising themselves as poor people in an affluent society often do.

CHAPTER TWENTY-ONE

Pizzo

IT took us two hours to walk to the coast. The vegetation changes startlingly as one nears the Tyrrhenian. Here lemon groves begin—avenues of aquarium-green shade—and the roads are lined with walls of prickly pear. Men were gathering the fruit as we passed and, glad of a rest, we stopped to watch them. Using a fork at the end of a long stick, they wrenched off the creamy orange eggs and then rubbed them on the road to get rid of the spines. Yet the reward for so much trouble is meagre— the fruit is insipid and full of pips, and if you do not hold it very gingerly you can spend a whole day picking the minute spines out of your hands.

The prickly pear is such a typical South Mediterranean plant that we think of it as an integral part of the landscape, yet its fleshy flippers were not always there. It was first brought to Spain from South America in the fifteenth century and from there it spread to North Africa, Italy and the eastern shores of the Mediterranean, carried by sailors who ate the fruit to combat scurvy. In many ways this strange plant is of great value in preserving cultivable land—along the road to Pizzo it served to protect the lemon trees from wind and spray. It strikes root in any dry crevice and is practically indestructible. On Etna the lava fields have been made into vineyards, thanks to the prickly pear: once it takes hold, it crumbles the lava and makes soil of it.

At midday we reached Pizzo, a town built on cliffs which fall sheer into the sea. The quays of the little harbour were crowded with loafers. One old shellback buttonholed us and began a recitation of his exploits, but he became so enmeshed in the intricacies of islands and archipelagos, transposing most of Indonesia to the Caribbean, that I suspected he was like the ferry-boat captain in Pagnol's play whose most daring venture had been to cross the port of Marseilles.

The beach, which was so small it could have been shovelled into three fair-sized sacks, was a mass of roasting flesh. Large mothers, their shifts ballooning about them, wallowed on their bellies in the shallows while their children paddled naked. Nobody ventured far out and the men, once they had plucked up enough courage to swim a short distance, stayed close together and kept shouting to conceal their nervousness. At one end of the beach we found a rocky promontory, unoccupied, and bathed there in the clear, tepid water.

Calabrians like company and our splendid isolation did not last long. Swimmers began to work up towards us and soon formed a protective circle, like porpoises round a stricken companion. The bobbing faces gulped out questions to which we gulped replies until, tired of such aqueous and unintelligible conversation, we suffered ourselves to be driven ashore.

Our triumphant pursuers—seven youths from the local *liceo*— had taken us for Germans, and seemed sorry to find that we did not come up to expectations. This did not daunt them, however, and the two leaders of the group launched into passionate praise of Germans and everything Germanic. I made it clear that personality and not nationality interested me, but they had got the bit between their teeth and were bent on taking us through the whole gamut of German splendours and achievements. It was obviously a lesson well learned, but when I pressed them to say why they personally admired the Teuton so much they could only reply, lamely, 'because they are such good soldiers.'

After escaping the boys on the beach we climbed back into the main square in search of a restaurant. On the way, another escort was forced upon us. Groups of youths appeared out of side streets; others left the café terraces where they had been sitting and followed us, plying us with questions. At last we found refuge in a trattoria. Even then they hung about the door for some time, the waiter winking encouragement at them. He was a surly specimen and pretended to be deeply shocked when I asked the price of the meal before sitting down.

'Eh, Riccardo. Do you hear that? They want to know the price! Whatever next!' Several heads appeared at the kitchen hatch to see the unruly customers who dared insist on value for money. No self-respecting tourist would act like that, surely?

Asking the price is a necessary precaution because, after a perfectly ordinary meal which could be summed up in the formula *primo, secondo e frutta*, you are often presented with an outrageous bill on which the simple items of the meal are analysed with the minuteness of an apothecary to prove that you have had many 'extras'. If you state your case clearly from the start, you have a good chance of getting a meal on the same footing as the regular customers.

Some regulars sitting near us heartily approved of my tactics and made great game of the waiter. Before we had finished eating they rose to go, and I noticed one of them was a pedlar. From behind the restaurant he wheeled a bicycle, or what had once been several bicycles, now held together by rust and string, and on that contraption were piled more things than could be got into a roomy van. A crazy assortment of scarves, ribbons and brassières was suspended from every side of the machine, and two suitcases stuffed with hardware were strapped on to the carrier. The man somehow threaded himself through all these trappings and, once in the saddle, raced away downhill with his swaying cargo.

These pedlars are usually men who have been unemployed for years. They often begin their career walking and carrying a bulging pack or suitcase, but, if business improves, they buy a bicycle or a hand-cart. Those who attain the height of perambulatory success even buy a motor-scooter and go chasing about the country with a trailer bouncing behind them. They are just some among thousands in South Italy who have to earn a living as jobbers, middlemen and factotums because they are unable to find permanent employment in an established enterprise. This is the result of the way in which Southern commerce is organised. Only four shops in the South have a staff of more than a hundred. Ninety-one per cent of the retail shops are owned and managed on a family basis—so that no one from outside has a chance of being employed there, unless he is content to earn a beggarly wage.

CHAPTER TWENTY-TWO

Foiled!

A CAR—your own car, that is—does not help you to meet people, but other people's cars can often provide interesting contacts. This time we were unlucky. It had been our intention to go up inland from Pizzo and explore the region of the Serre, but fate decreed otherwise.

The road to Serra San Bruno is a bad road, little frequented at any time. We had been walking along it for over an hour when two men offered us a lift. I understood that they were going to Monterosso—a village slightly off our route, though still in the right direction—but they drove on for a good five miles and then suddenly pulled up beside a quarry in a deserted valley. I asked for explanations and they said they had to wait by the road until a building contractor, who was working on a nearby site, came to give them some money.

'Don't worry. He will only be half an hour or so and when he comes we will take you on down the coast to Bagnara.' All this seemed very improbable, as well as disquieting, for Bagnara was seventy miles away in the other direction.

I told them that we wanted to go to Serra San Bruno, but they pooh-poohed the idea. 'What do you want to go there for? There is nothing to see!' They themselves had never been there. Calabrians have a reputation for being stubborn, but these two were hand-picked mules.

We waited and waited. There was no sign of any contractor and not one car passed going in the direction we wanted to take. This meant we had to talk, though I didn't like either of the men.

Both were married. One was about thirty, slight and nervous, given to laughing hysterically. The other was fifty, boorish and argumentative. They asked if we were Catholics. 'No.' A dark look from the elder man. 'Huh. You must be Protestants, then.' 'No.' 'But that's impossible. Everyone is either Catholic or Protestant. Anyway, how did you manage to get married if you don't go to church?' I explained the workings of that happy institution, civil marriage, and added that marriage out of church was also possible in Italy. This they flatly refused to believe (news of the 1958 Prato incident, in which civil marriage was temporarily vindicated by the courts, despite ecclesiastical opposition, had evidently never spread as far as Bagnara) and angrily asserted that we were trying to propagate subversion.

Two hours had passed and we were still awaiting the arrival of the mythical personage with the money. One car, going the right way, came along just before dusk, but was absolutely full. Should we camp on the spot? Mosquitoes swarmed everywhere; there was no village for miles and we had nothing to eat.

'You see,' they jeered, 'you will have to come with us!'

A labourer appeared on his bicycle to say that the contractor had not been in the vicinity for two days. The men swore and backed the car furiously, ready to make for the coast road again. It was a sad defeat, but we agreed to go back as far as Pizzo, and no farther, to buy food. I was a fool to trust them. They drove straight through Pizzo, ignoring all entreaties to stop.

'Never you mind,' said the younger man. 'We know a place where you can camp at Bagnara. You will be all right there.' Short of jumping out of the car, which was travelling at a steady eighty, there was nothing much we could do.

I doubt if one person in ten thousand in Southern Italy has so much as seen a tent and the last thing to do is to rely on the advice of locals when looking for a place to camp. Once, on arriving at nightfall in a small town near Naples, I was assured by a passer-by that he knew just the place for my tent. I woke

151

next morning in what I had fondly imagined to be a large park and found a crowd of people staring at me. I had been sleeping under one of four trees in a public square, and that very tree had been selected by some tramps as a place to leave their litter and respond amply to the promptings of nature.

While such thoughts, and worse, were going through my mind we arrived in Vibo Valentia. The town had been plunged into darkness, owing to a power failure. There the two madcaps stopped and entered a bar lit by candles. Everybody seemed to know them and the cashier gave us some very meaningful looks. I had been wondering from the beginning who the two men were, and the way the cashier frowned at me over the top of his glasses convinced me that it was time to bring our jaunt to an end. 'So they have caught you, too, have they?' he seemed to be saying. 'You ought to have more sense.'

There was no point in being too brusque if we wanted to get away, so we sat at a table with the men and ordered beer and sandwiches. A young woman was standing near the bar and, at the invitation of the man with the falsetto laugh, she came and joined us. She was short and stocky but with pretty, irregular features. At first she played the prude, giggling, edging away from the man who was trying to pinch her thigh, but no girl could have resisted the atmosphere of candlelight for long with the summer night calling outside. She listened to him, let his hand rove, fixed him with her unwavering black eyes. They began to talk earnestly in hot, breathy whispers while the other man leaned back, guzzled his beer and winked at us.

Finally she agreed to let them take her to her village on the road to Mileto—she had apparently missed the last bus—and this gave me the opportunity of saying that we would get out at the same village and spend the night there. This statement produced no response. Now that an unaccompanied woman had come into the picture we were ignored; this suited me very well.

The five of us piled into the car—I kept hoping against hope that our belongings were still in the boot—and went pelting through the deserted suburbs. The woman was wedged in between the two men on the front seat. They both fondled her, in so far as space would permit, and while they were kissing her she chattered away about her family. 'I've got a husband and two children. He is away but . . . I'm married, I'm married.' They laughed at her and cracked smutty jokes at her expense. 'And does your husband know you earn your money lying on your back?' asked the boorish man.

It seemed a long time before the car stopped in a narrow village street lit by sulphurous orange lamps. I had almost fallen asleep, but the slam of the car doors brought me up with a start and I leaped out to recover our bags.

The two men began pleading again: 'Come on with us to Bagnara. What are you going to do here?' But we walked away up the street with the girl clopping along beside us. Stumbling over her words and trembling—though the night was not cold—she explained how we were to find our way out of the village.

'Just before you go, tell me who those men were,' I said.

'I don't know, I don't know,' she said, flustered.

'But you must know. They told you, didn't they?'

And then she lifted up her face and I saw her eyes narrow and harden. 'Yes, I know them. Business men from Bagnara, they call themselves. *Gente cattiva*! A good thing for you you got out here!' She ran off down a side street, keeping close to the wall. Her steps echoed in the stillness; she did not look back.

There was no moon and, once we had left the village, it was as much as we could do to distinguish the road. The stones under our feet were the only certainty. Suddenly there were olive trees rustling and then a bank loomed up, just outlined against the sky. At the top of the bank there was a ploughed field to cross and, at its far edge, a lone tree. There we lay down to sleep.

Not long before dawn I woke under the canopy of the mulberry tree. From a cart-track that ran behind the field came the clip-clop of many pairs of wooden shoes. The hedge rustled; faces peered over. A group of workmen let out a gasp of surprise. For a long time they stared without saying a word, then one of them sprinted away. He came back after a few minutes with a bunch of grapes which he handed to us, shyly. 'This is for your breakfast. If you want water I will show you where to find it.'

Calabrians help you in a disconcerting way. It is simply something which has to be done and they are surprised if you thank them. Our thanks, then, were addressed to backs only. The men were already walking away, gravely, heads held high.

Our limbs ached. The grapes were sour. Hills, misted with olive trees, spread away eastwards. Some channels of shadow still lingered—groves of pomegranates and figs. The earth was honey-warm in the early sun.

A fair-haired boy had come to finish ploughing the field. He fitted a net on the head of his ox to prevent the flies bothering it and, as he spoke to it in his reedy voice, the great dun creature raised its muzzle and lolloped out its tongue to thank him.

The workman soon came back as he had promised. He was a tall, gangling fellow with a fixed smile. On his shoulder he carried the largest amphora I have ever seen. 'And that only lasts us the morning. I have to fill it again after lunch. It's thirsty work digging trenches for a pipe-line!'

A cistern at the bottom of the hill, crumbling among the knotted roots of a fig-tree, was full of soapy water that drained into a garden where maize and tomatoes grew. The pump gave a hollow, sucking sound and produced a mere trickle. An old woman, sinewy and rank-smelling, came to wash clothes. She was followed by a fat dame who stared so much at us that she kept forgetting the linen, which slipped into the greasy tank and had to be drubbed all over again.

The disappointment of having missed the Serre still rankled

but, as it was too far to go back, we decided to move on down the coast. It took us all the morning, walking briskly, to reach Gioia Tauro, where we stopped for a snack. Gioia is a drab town of one long street lined with two-storeyed houses, yet it must be a prosperous place. The plain of Rizziconi in which it stands contains some of the finest olive trees in Italy and most of the lemons and oranges in Calabria are grown in the region. From Gioia to Palmi the road runs through orchards and groves of eucalyptus.

A Neapolitan on his way to Sicily took us to Palmi. I imagined he was going on holiday. 'Holiday be blowed! My wife and children are waiting for me. I don't need to read about the cold war in the newspapers—I live it at home every day!' He looked narrowly at me. 'You are young and you've got a fine girl there. Take my advice; don't have children too early.'

It is so rare to hear an Italian advise against having children that I laughed out loud. He didn't see the joke.

'But I'm serious! Do you think we should be living as we do now if we didn't have so many children? This country is being strangled with an umbilical cord!'

These dark musings were sometimes interrupted by whoops, garbled phrases in English and sudden fits of shrill whistling. At one point the car made straight for the yawning door of a church that sat solidly in the middle of the road. 'Hats off! Here we go!' We shaved the corner on two wheels and just slipped under the nose of a big trailer coming up from Reggio.

'There you are. A good thing I heard him coming. It would have taken us a quarter of an hour to get through that gap—and they call it a main road! Talk, talk, talk—years of it! The church must go—everybody says so—but here churches never go; not even that monstrosity. Mind you, it must be grand to pile up outside a church. They carry you in, candles ready. . . .' We were quite glad to reach Palmi.

It is a pleasant place, but we did not stop. It was full of tourists and had something of the glee-club atmosphere which pervades other towns along the Tyrrhenian coast. We preferred to travel inland again.

CHAPTER TWENTY-THREE

A Backwater

FROM the coast the road winds steeply towards the foothills of Aspromonte. Overhanging plane trees made the way cool and easy at first—but it was three o'clock, an hour when any mortal should be at rest on a summer's day in Calabria, and we became tired just when the planes were no longer accompanying us. Olive trees took over, cavernous and with trunks so thick that you could not put both arms round them. We went to join them where they dozed in the yellow grass.

The mountain wind woke us. A sudden flurry of colour in the sunlight attracted my attention: two birds on a telegraph wire. From time to time they glided down, hovered over a field, searching, tacking, stabbing with curved beaks, and then floated upwards in long, swinging curves to perch again on the wire. They were bee-eaters. One sees few birds in Calabria in summer, and I doubt whether there are many to be seen at any time. The people shoot anything that flies.

One more mile and we reached Seminara. The village was decorated with lanterns and festal arches for the pilgrimage which takes place there every year. At first sight it looked gay, but no amount of decoration could hide its real character—a skeleton garlanded with coloured streamers. In the main square the workless were rousing up from the benches under the acacias where they had been sleeping all the afternoon and were wandering among the stalls which had been set up for the fête. These contained nothing but hideous china horses, balloons with demon faces and mounds of fly-covered *torrone*.

If the square was heartening, the back streets left us no illusions. Most of the houses were wooden shacks; those that had any appearance of solidity looked like piles of mud. A few might once have been almost presentable, but now the walls were leprous, the grilles rusty, the shutters warped. All were crumbling; all stank. The stench was particularly overpowering near the church, the gathering place of pilgrims, because the paved courtyard which surrounds it is used as a public lavatory—people can crouch and chat in comfort there. The flight of steps leading to the side door was covered with dried turds, and two men snored drunkenly against the main porch.

Outside one ruin of a house we stopped to take a photograph. The cobbler who lived there invited us inside to look over his workshop. It contained his workbench, two chairs and a cupboard. The ceiling was low and smoke-blackened and, despite the tang of leather and wax, the room smelled strongly of dirty linen and stale food. The cobbler wore a green jersey and a brown apron and, with his long grey hair and spade beard, made a biblical figure. He spoke haltingly, heaving the words from his chest, and fixed you with burning eyes as he spoke. From the bench he brought a pair of shoes, just finished.

'I make them. They are good shoes, but everybody buys shoes from the Northern factories now because they are cheaper. I carry on, though, and manage to sell a pair or two every month. It is my life. I would make shoes even if nobody bought them.' He caressed the leather thoughtfully but, with all his craftsman's pride, he looked dejected and careworn—as if, in paring away each strip of leather, he was paring away his own being which fell as so many useless shavings to his feet.

The stairs creaked. There was a timid rattle at the latch and a young girl peeped through the door.

'This is my daughter. The mother is dead, God rest her soul.' As the girl stood hesitating he became impatient. 'Don't stand there gaping, Livia. These people would like to speak to you.' She was round-faced, awkward, and when she looked at her father there was fear in her heifer-eyes. No chance for her to flower among people of her own age; no hob-nobbing outside the house. She was her father's sole companion and he spoke to her as if she was his servant.

We had photographed the house and so, before we left, we had to photograph them. There was an embarrassing moment when we asked for their address. The old man could not write, so I offered to write for him. 'Oh, no. Livia can write. Give her your note-book.' The poor girl was little better than her father. Ducking her head so that her blushes should not be seen, she took nearly five minutes to write their address in an almost illegible hand.

Feeling very hungry, we drifted back into the square on the look-out for a restaurant. A jovial individual, covered with flour from head to foot, came out of a bakery and hailed us. 'Trattoria? There isn't one, but wait a minute, I know the very thing for you!' He hurried into the shop and then emerged again, without his flour-mantle. 'Follow me. I'll take you somewhere where you will get a good meal.'

Down another murky lane we went, past piles of glazed pots that had cascaded out of a yard. Though Seminara is renowned for its pottery, these were disappointing—all lizard-green and yellow. The baker entered a small store which purported to be a grocery, though it was full of nothing but bags of peas and lentils. He bustled through into the back shop. A man writing at a table rose and grunted some words of greeting. He was very tall and heavily-built and his horn-rimmed spectacles gave him an owlish, schoolmasterly air. Though he tried to be polite he was obviously surprised and angry at the intrusion. The breezy baker slapped him on the back.

'These people want something to eat. You'll set them up all right, won't you?' The shopkeeper agreed, much against his will, and the baker left us, saying he would return in an hour to see if we had eaten.

The dark, narrow room was filthy. The threadbare oilcloth

on the table was covered with food stains. The cane-bottomed chairs were holed and nipped our posteriors. A wall cupboard, which hung awry, was crammed with an inextricable muddle of rags, chipped crockery, match-boxes and artificial flowers, all ready to fall on to the floor. Above the cupboard were some fly-blown photographs of family ghosts in sepia and over a soiled and rumpled bed hung a strange visionary painting with a touch of Chagall about it.

There was a clatter of saucepans, followed by muttered curses. From the black hole of a kitchen, separated from the living-room by a greasy chintz curtain, came the mother. Her emaciated face and matted black hair made it impossible to tell her age, but she could not have been more than thirty-five. She ignored us completely and fell to scolding her husband and her daughters. One daughter, a frumpish, sour-faced girl, served in the shop. The other, a frail creature, sat at the table, her eyes riveted on an exercise book in which she was copying letters.

After a lot of bickering the mother fussed off into the kitchen. The man asked us what we wanted to eat.

'We have got plenty of lentils, but if you want some meat I shall have to go out and buy it.' This he proceeded to do, leaving us to count the flies and talk to the doe-eyed girl who swung her spindle legs beneath the chair and made great efforts with capitals and small to impress the visitors.

It was a long time before he lumbered back, carrying in his hand a piece of meat which looked as though it had hit the dust on its way from the butcher's. The meat was passed through the curtain and, when it began to sizzle, he turned his attention to us. He was no conversationalist; words somehow stuck in his throat. After making a few remarks about the weather he was reduced to gulping hard and taking occasional swipes at some kittens which were locked in combat on the bed. He next busied himself laying the table and opened the refrigerator—a most incongruous object in that room—to bring out a bottle of beer.

A stony silence prevailed during most of the meal. We all ate together and were joined by a little boy, the son of the family, who had just come in from work. They told me he was a potter's apprentice, but it seemed unusual to find any sort of apprentice aged ten. While we fought with the tough meat and bone-dry lentils, they ate a small plate of olives, a hunk of bread and a cup of transparent soup. The children were given a biscuit each as dessert. There was no fruit and no fresh green-stuff, the refrigerator being used only for drinks.

Our attempts at talking with the children met with no success. They sat conning over their plates and replied in monosyllables. At last the silence was broken by the return of the baker. Whether he thought he had done his friends a good turn by taking us there, I don't know, but he looked very disappointed when he saw the circle of churchyard faces and soon set about trying to dispel the gloom. 'What do I see! Haven't they given you any fruit? We'll soon fix that.' He drew two pears from his pocket and rolled them into the middle of the table.

He turned out to be an unholy leg-puller and a great drinker. Delianova was his home town, but he claimed to have seen everything worth seeing in the world. His stories were all in the same vein—grossly exaggerated accounts of his numerous conquests, which included a 'delicious nun' and an 'Arabian gazelle' whom he had seduced while on very active service in Libya.

'I hate drinking,' he said, after the fifth bottle of beer, 'but I have to make a sacrifice so that people like these can live.' The wife raised a wintry smile, but the husband continued to look angry and bored.

This one-man performance was amusing in its early stages, but he rambled on and on until his verbal flux became as disquieting as the previous silence had been. After an hour he decided his time had come to shift to another café where he might find a more appreciative audience, but he made it clear that he did not want to lose sight of us. 'Meet me later in the bakery. We'll have a drink and then you can sleep in my room.'

It was getting late and we wanted to leave the village before dark. I settled the bill and rose to go. The father took me into a cupboard under the stairs where, if you were prepared to double yourself into an S shape, you could wash in a cracked, hair-clotted bowl round which were pasted garish pictures of languid beauties and mountain landscapes.

We were making for the door when the poor, jaded mother dashed forward and kissed L on both cheeks. She stood back, gazing silently at us. Her mouth puckered up and she began to cry in short, choking gasps. 'God, oh God! No foreigners have ever been to this house before. And to think we received you like this!'

I was glad to leave Seminara. The same olive trees gave us hospitality for the night and next morning we made our way back to Palmi.

CHAPTER TWENTY-FOUR

Law and Order

A HIGH cliff rises to the south of Palmi. If you climb its grassy back—it takes almost an hour—you can see the yawning bay of Gioia, the Straits and the Aeolian islands. We arrived early, before the sun had drawn all colour into itself. Below the water was green, but from there it stretched away, blue sapphire and creamy floss, to where the islands cruised, hull-down.

Coming to the sea again was like returning to freedom. The land does not satisfy so consistently because it has been changed by man—the bones are poking through its flesh. An hour passed, perhaps two, watching the sea. We paid for our lapse of consciousness by having to eat in a classy restaurant with a coach-load of Milanese bound for Sicily.

That afternoon we reached Bagnara. The mountains hardly give the town a chance to breathe. On the sheer slopes, which plunge almost into the streets, are terraced vineyards no more than a yard wide. For most of the year Bagnara is a sleepy place, though it boils with activity in May and June when the sword-fish come to the coast from Arctic waters. All along the shore there are towers from which a watch is kept to assist the boats in intercepting the shoals. Bagnara has a reputation as a smuggling town; the plain which lies south of it is well known for the acts of banditry committed there after the last war. This, if one wishes to believe all the tales that are told, is now 'bandits' corner' since the famous brigands of the Sila and Aspromonte are all below ground.

Popular novelists in many countries have exercised their talents in describing the dark deeds perpetrated by Calabrian and Sicilian bandits; the romantic aura with which they have been invested still wears well. Lawlessness, in fact, was the inevitable result of the popular struggle, first against foreign domination and later against the central government established after the unification of Italy.

For the people of the South, Rome is the place where the big-wigs live—those who exploit but who never deign to come and see for themselves—and the Southerners have an innate distrust of officialdom. Hopes have so often been raised by officials brimming over with good intentions, only to be left to rot in some ministry drawer. So people have reacted in two ways—they have either revolted or shrunk into themselves. South Italy's trade unions have no real power, and there is no traditional belief that, if you protest long and loudly enough, your claims will eventually receive attention. The result is a complete lack of civic sense and co-operation. Individualism is either pushed to excess, so contributing little to common profit, or forced to stagnate. The peasants and workers have great inventive powers and take pride in their work, yet all goes to waste because lethargic bosses give them no encouragement. I heard of a dyer in a factory in Calabria who found new dyes and methods through making experiments of his own. He told the factory owner, who dismissed the suggestions out of hand as being useless. The secret was jealously guarded—even the dyer's workmates did not know of his discoveries—and it will always remain so.

The peasant personalises everything. An old man in Lucania said to me one day: 'This field where I am working is not mine, nor is the donkey, nor is the plough. But they *are* mine, really, because I know and love them—the master doesn't.'

Not long ago, in Calabria, an incident occurred which illustrates the state of mind of those to whom law and order means either exploitation or total neglect. A train travelling to Catanzaro fell from a bridge into a gorge and many of the passengers were killed. The reaction of the bereaved and of their friends was immediate—they all went to Catanzaro and proceeded to smash up the town hall and the police station. In their view, the authorities were directly responsible for the accident. There must be some deep and long-standing grievance if people can convince themselves that their lives are wilfully endangered.

CHAPTER TWENTY-FIVE

Jasmine Coast

SCILLA lives up to its reputation. The rock and the deserted shingle beach glowed in the afternoon sun; webs of light quivered over the rocks offshore. The coast southwards is one rolling flood of orange and lemon trees, and here, too, the bergamot first appears. This tree, which is hardly distinguishable from the lemon and has identical fruit, grows only on the narrow strip of land extending from Villa San Giovanni to Cape Spartivento, a distance of some sixty miles.

Near Santa Trada, where a towering pylon carries electric cables across to Punta del Faro on the Sicilian side, we stopped for the night. A tall ship passed down the fairway—Alexandria, Bombay. The dusk stole in from the east; Messina rippled into light on the far shore.

Next day we arrived in Reggio. The streets are full of Semitic faces. The girls walk in laughing groups on one side; the men barge along on the other, staring fiercely. When they look at you, you feel that a fully loaded revolver is being aimed at your head. Reggio is the largest city in Calabria; its streets are rushing waves of sound. It is hot, sweet-smelling, and gradually, as you wander, the smells become separate and distinct. Women's perfume, sweat and dust predominate, but there is the odour of roasting sausages, fried calamary, hot bread, wine, jasmine, incense and carnations. Black horse-drawn cabs with crazy concertina hoods bowl along the Corso—and, because the inhabitants have a habit of shouldering everyone off the pavement, you are likely to find the tasselled head of a cabhorse butting you in the back and the cabman's whip whistling about your ears.

We fought our way through the river of people towards the station in search of a hotel, but had no success. In a haberdasher's an old lady took me for her grandson and gave me a resounding kiss. When she had recovered from her surprise she gave us the address of a hotel which she thought would suit our requirements. We found it in a deserted back street near the port. In a courtyard, surrounded by a warren of cell-like rooms, a free-for-all was going on between some brawny washerwomen who were all trying to reach a tap to do their rinsing. Some of them would have been very much the worse for wear had not the manageress, a woman who sported a fine moustache and who was as wide as she was high, emerged from her private quarters to restore order. When the shouting had subsided she marched us upstairs.

Flinging open the door of a cold, musty room, she stared into its cavernous depths and pronounced the formula which I suppose she used for all her guests. 'Do you want it for an hour or for the night?' I would not have wanted it for ten minutes. It was decorated in red and black and would have made a good anteroom to hell. The old witch had sadly miscalculated if she imagined that Venus would feel at home in such a lurid setting—but, then, perhaps the locals are not so particular.

Eventually we found accommodation in a hotel right at the other end of the town. There the manageress asked if we were Germans, and, on being assured that we were not, she gave us the only room available which was large and clean. The luxury of a bed that night after so long!

Quite early in the morning the room began to vibrate and ominous growlings came from the other side of the wall. It was not, as I had imagined, Mount Etna rousing from its slumbers, but simply the geyser in action in the bathroom.

The landlady's discrimination of the night before did not

spring from any personal predilection for one breed of foreigner as opposed to another. We were presented with a preposterous bill and, during the argument which followed, the truth came out. She had asked if we were Germans because, a few days previously, some Germans had kicked up a fuss and threatened to go to the police when she overcharged them. If she thought we were made of meeker stuff, she was wrong. I sought out the husband and, after going through the items together, we arrived at a figure which resembled the authorised tariff. In all fairness I must say that people seldom tried to cheat us while we were in Calabria. In the average shop they sell very little and so are attentive to customers, though without being over-insistent or smiling too commercial a smile.

The sister city, Messina, has stolen a march on Reggio. It is there that all the liners call; they even have a Salvatore standing in the sea to welcome them. The port of Reggio has no Salvatore and little deep-sea traffic. There are sailors on the quays, of course, but it is hard to look burly and play the old salt when your cargo is perfume and lemons. The ferry-boat makes a show; it is high and portly. One day it will be replaced. In fact, there is plenty of wishful thinking on both sides of the straits: they actually sell postcards which show a splendid but non-existent bridge.

A café terrace made a good vantage point for watching Reggio stretch its legs. Nannies, buckled into absurd uniforms, airing their charges, moved in a form of quadrille, outflanking the mountains of balloons bumping along the esplanade. A naval man, blancoed to set your teeth on edge, sprawled in a wicker chair beside us. He kept waggling his little finger furiously in one ear and clawing at his hairy calves. The girls were out again, fresher than the night before, firm as pillars in their lilac and yellow dresses. A barrel-organ appeared, groaning on splayed wheels. Its master tugged it, coaxed it, finally kicked it from behind, and it began to tinkle in spasms.

Our morning was to be spent at the museum. To reach it we took the back streets, mere slits between houses, choked with crucified shirts and wind-swollen combinations. Women in dressing-gowns screamed from high up among the washing, bird-cages and flower boxes.

There were girls, none of them much over sixteen, soliciting in doorways and men inviting us into restaurants to sample 'genuine sword-fish', which, on closer inquiry, proved to be imported from Japan.

The museum of Magna Graecia, which contains a wonderful collection of objects found in the South, was only opened to the public in 1958. The past of Southern Italy, unlike its present, has not been neglected, but all the treasures now exhibited were formerly in private collections. The government has recently seen fit to gather them under one roof.

Excavations in Calabria, Lucania and Puglia began relatively late. Most of the work has been concentrated at Cape Colonna and Locri so that, up to now, Sibari and Metaponto have been forgotten. This tardy revelation of what the Greeks left behind them is due to lack of government sponsorship. While no expense was spared for excavation in Campania and Sicily, discoveries were only made in 'Greater Greece' because of private initiative. Many of the local aristocrats were passionately interested in archaeology and themselves searched for the treasures which they believed lay beneath their lands.

We spent many hours in the museum and I doubt if we saw a quarter of all there is to see. The visit was marred to some extent by an over-diligent attendant who followed us about like a sleuth from the moment we entered the building. It was no good escaping upstairs and doubling round the pillars—he caught us every time, though in the end he began to puff and blow. At last I asked him why he insisted on snooping.

'These are my orders,' he said. 'It's a new place and . . . one never knows.' There is no denying that one of those Greek pots would make a fine tea-caddy.

There is a river marked on the map to the south of Reggio. It turned out to be completely dry and full of piles of rubbish where dogs rooted in search of scraps. Between the piles, which were burning slowly, sat groups of boys tending the fires. To pass the time they were playing knucklebones—juggling with a skeleton. Up went the bones, flashing in the sun, and down again to land on small brown hands. The cries of the children mingled with the yapping and growling of a dog worrying a piece of rag; the suffocating smoke billowed lazily up the river-bed.

It was a long walk out of the town; the heat was like a sledge-hammer. Outside a church we stopped and rested in the porch. Within five minutes as many people had come to tell us we were wasting our time if we expected to get a lift, but then a minicar pulled up under the astonished gaze of those who had predicted failure. The driver filled the front of the car, but we squeezed into the back and sat doubled up on some oilcans.

Fat people are often jovial, but this man's heartiness was forced and he had a horrible sadistic smile. As I watched him steering with his belly, he made me think of an evil, outsize octopus. The usual kind of argument began as we neared Melito: 'What are you going to Melito for? There is nothing to see there. Come with me to Bova. I've got a villa on the beach!'

I insisted on stopping at Melito and the man became angry.

'Ah! You are gypsies, are you? Don't want to be in a civilised place, I suppose.'

He took us beyond Melito and drew up near a railway bridge where, ironically enough, there was a gipsy camp.

'Here you are. This is the place for you. Go and join them and good luck to you!' Heaving with laughter and gritting his teeth, he drove away, leaving us on the scalding hot road. The sirocco was blowing and the waves churned on the beach below the gipsy camp. They were sitting under their tent but, when they saw us, two of them ran up near the road and begged us to throw down cigarettes.

Melito was not very far behind. Its white houses peeped through the prickly pear and giant aloes. As we walked back we fell in with a girl who was carrying a pink sunshade. She was as fresh as cinnamon and moved like a queen. 'I'm from Bova Interior. I'm going into town to see my brother who is in hospital.'

Having heard about the Greek-speaking colonies in the mountains, I asked her if she knew any Greek. 'I understand it, but I can't speak. My parents can, though, and do you know when they use it?' She laughed and her eyes glistened. 'When they are in a love mood!' The mystery of these Greeks in the Aspromonte has never been solved. Some think they came with the Albanians, while others are convinced that they are descendants of the ancient Greek colonists.

The towns inside Calabria have grown out of the rock, are rock itself. Those on the coast are drugged by the sea, as Melito is, but what it lacks in vitality it makes up for in colour. Behind the flat-roofed houses, though not jostling them, the mountains rise, ginger and smoke-grey. Palms and bananas shade the tangled gardens, bougainvillea spills out over every wall and jasmine ruffles its myriad stars. The dome of orange bignonia that almost hides the hospital makes the whole town smell of roast coffee. Coffee and salt—just at the end of the main street is the beach.

Some bougainvillea swept us into a restaurant. 'Si accomodi, per favore!' We were served with as much delay as possible by a squint-eyed girl who put on a good show of being stone deaf. This meant keeping up a series of running skirmishes with the kitchen until the last peach stone, sucked clean, shone on our plates.

The hospital garden looked cool and inviting for an after-dinner rest. Some doctors saw us go in, mumbled *forestieri*, and let us wander, but we were caught by a pregnant woman, her husband and mother who were sitting on a bench. 'Are you married? Have you any children? Are you

Catholics?' Not again! We fled from their bath-robes and importunities and sought refuge on a log near the garden wall.

Just as I was settling down to a session of note-writing, a young man came to sit on the log beside us. He stared, shuffled his feet, coughed. For once we did not want to talk and we were holding out well when a lad sprang up, bearing a tray of coffee. These white-jacketed coffee imps haunt every Calabrian town. They are sent round from cafés to solicit card-players, those who have just had a nap—anyone, in fact, in a sitting or recumbent posture whom they should happen to come across. They plant themselves in front of you and hypnotise you with eyes like the cups of coffee they carry. If you show a flicker of weakness a cup is thrust into your hand, followed by a glass of water, for they always have two trays—one for the coffee, the other spread with glasses of water to cool your mouth.

We were offered some coffee, capitulated and had to talk. The young man's expression was distressingly vacant, but he proved to be a quiet, thoughtful fellow. He had a resounding Greek name and was very proud of it.

'I work as a garage-hand in Crotone; eight hours a day. Every year I change my job because, when I ask for a holiday, I am kicked out. That's how it goes here. Officially, of course, everyone gets paid holidays. The point is, you are lucky if you can keep the same job two years running.' His sympathies were with the Communists but, though sputniks had impressed him, he was chary of power-politics. 'They make gods of all the statesmen, as if they were anything but clowns! I hate to think our future depends on such people.'

A nurse called from a window high up in the hospital. 'I must go. Injection time.' He walked slowly away, head bent.

The oleanders hung limp on the deserted station platform; the wind had dropped. The beach was on the other side of the railway line, clean grey sand which dipped to the sea in a ridge of pebbles. Farther out were rocks studded with anemones which trembled on each drag of water. Droves of dappled fishes raced in the shallows.

The afternoon wore on. Nobody came. Terns skimmed in screaming packs over the sleeping sea. At the far end of the beach was a nest of fishing boats. Towards sunset men appeared and began to busy themselves with the tackle, and we went to watch them put out. One of the boats was owned by six brothers, only two of whom were sober. These spent all their time trying to prevent the other four from blundering among the nets.

The sea grew violet. Etna blurred in plumes of mist. One boat was launched, leaving a silver snail's wake on the quiet water. Women came running to the shore and, lifting their skirts high, waded out and sprang abroad to join their men.

The brothers were preparing to go lantern fishing. 'A doctor is going with us,' they said. 'He is from Rome.' The doctor appeared, accompanied by two girls in trousers. They spoke to the fishermen as if they were children, and the fishermen pretended to enjoy being patronised. 'No room for you in the boat,' cried the girls. 'We *are* sorry!'

A boy who was standing nearby offered to row us out a short way—'just for a taste of salt'. He was seventeen, bright-eyed, awkward. His main interest in life, apart from fishing, was cowboy and gangster films. He told me that the fishermen earn most of their money in spring and autumn. For a good catch they get thirty thousand lire—anchovies and mullet are the money-bringers—and when they have had several good catches they stop working for a month or two. 'We could earn more, but what would we do with the money?'

It was almost dark when our boat crunched on to the pebbles. Warm voices and volleys of laughter came from groups of people who were preparing to sleep on the beach. A lighted lamp hung from the prow of each boat; the nets were ready. Women came to peer at us. There was a flutter of surprise and whispering. 'They are foreigners!' The women turned away without a word.

We went back along the beach past the church, the Virgin of Porto Salvo, which, with its lights, guides mariners at night. The fishing boats crept along the shore and then made for the open sea. Their lanterns slowly dwindled and reddened—a shoal of fire-flies riding into darkness. The beach shook with the throb of a liner that passed like a blazing castle up the straits.

The night was balmy with the scent of jasmine from the nearby perfume factory. We slept on waves of sand, under the whirling stars. At three o'clock in the morning some fishermen trudged by, hauling nets, and stopped when they saw us. Were we asleep, dead, spirits? With quavering voices they called: *'Cristiani, siete Cristiani?'* We replied sleepily that we were not of the other world and they went on their way. A Christian—that means a human being to them.

Next morning the train from Taranto came through and left a smudge of smoke on the face of dawn. The white church caught the first splash of sun when the jagged hand of Pentedattilo was still in shadow. The fishing boats were all drawn up on the shore as if they had never stirred.

This was the last dawn we saw in Calabria. That morning we crossed to Messina and looked back at cloudy Aspromonte. The sky was white and full of gulls wheeling.

Vale

In October 1964 something important happened in the Mezzogiorno: the 468-mile *Autostrada del Sole* from Milan to Salerno was completed. This four-lane highway, the first of its kind to link North and South, is significant not only because it symbolises the continuation of the Roman tradition of road building, but also because it represents the desire of the Italian government to make North and South one political and economic unit. Significant, too, is the fact that the highway was begun from the northern end, though the plan is to extend it as far as Reggio and, possibly, Palermo.

Nobody can deny that an effort has been made to improve conditions in the South since 1950; but, though thirty-eight per cent of the people of Italy live in Il Mezzogiorno, they still get only twenty-one per cent of the national income. The considerable industrialisation over the past years has been concentrated in Campania and Sicily where the main trend has been in petrol and chemicals. Calabria and Lucania have hardly come into the industrial picture as yet—though, very recently, natural gas was found in central Lucania and wells have been sunk at Pisticci to provide energy for a new petrochemical plant.

The problem, in fact, is not so much one of the number of new factories or of the increase in production. It is the attitude towards the people of the South which is important. Cavour once said something to the effect that Italy and the Italians had to be 'made'. This process is still going on, and it implies uniformity imposed from above, the very thing which the

Southerner has always resisted.   Since the war the Mezzogiorno has been treated as an under-developed region which has to be welded on to the North.

People will tell you quite openly that the South is a potential gold mine because of its low labour costs.   Attempts to relieve poverty still hark back to the old charitable methods of the Church or, in modern dress, become American and paternal— a sop to the destitute.   Much money is spent on what is new and impressive, no matter if it turns out to be uneconomic; and, as most investment comes from Northern industrialists, profits will inevitably flow back to Northern banks.

When they hear South Italy mentioned, most people think of sun and sentimental songs: to them it is the realm of the happy-go-lucky.   Those who are concerned with social problems, the specialists, think of poverty: they make a diagnosis and suggest a cure.   I hope I have done nothing to confirm popular impressions which still smack of the nineteenth century.   Though I am interested in the conditions in the South, I am not an economist. My aim has simply been to show how these conditions affect individuals, for it is they who matter.

In Mediterranean lands one still finds an attitude to life which is whole and unreserved.   The people may not be complex, but they are all of a piece, growing from the inside like a rock. Their non-conformity is genuine because it is unconscious. Their realism may appear brash, but that is because, instead of worrying about reality, they live it.   This, among many other things, is what attracts us and makes us wish to return again and again to the inland sea: it is a way of re-discovering simplicity.

PRINTED IN THE U.S.A.

1/14/67

51920

DG
975
C15
G8

GUNNELL, BRYN
    CALABRIAN SUMMER.

DATE DUE	
AUG - 5 1997	

Fernald Library
Colby Sawyer College
New London, New Hampshire

GAYLORD   PRINTED IN U.S.A.